A Conviction Based Upon Lies

Matthew Pugh

Edited by Kevin L. Epps

Cadmus Publishing
www.cadmuspublishing.com

Copyright © 2022 Matthew Pugh

Cover art by Tad M. Bomboli

Published by Cadmus Publishing
www.cadmuspublishing.com
Port Angeles, WA

ISBN: 978-1-63751-279-1

DEDICATION

This book is dedicated to my mother, father, and my grandparents. For your love, support, and leadership, which has given me the willingness to believe in my faith within my soul so that I could forever move in this life with this higher power in the heat of battles to overcome self, remain calm and reach a greater success.

There are a number of ways to see the corruption involved in this case. As I sat in a state of calm while being sentenced, my mindset was preparing for solitude. When a man becomes great, he becomes solitary. He goes into solitude. To seek, and that which he seeks he finds, for there is a way to all knowledge, all wisdom, all truth, all power. This allowed me to connect the loopholes included in this injustice.

-Matthew Pugh

PREFACE

This book is not your average read about court proceedings and rules of law. I will portray a vision of my experience and perception to give insight of this unfair trial and how I managed to handle these governmental officials in a position of power. Sometimes when a situation or circumstance looks defeated, usually it is just the beginning of victory.

These nineteen chapters of my mindset contained in the writing of this book will be intense, raw, shocking, clever, gritty, honest, surprisingly different, compelling, powerful, organic, and will leave you wanting more! You will come to understand how and why I could maintain my composure after receiving sixty years and chose to read The Power of Positive Thinking by Norman Vincent Peale as my former attorney showed signs of defeat. Sometimes, the grim reality awakens the soul to fight for what is right.

"First, they ignore you.
Then, they laugh at you.
Then, they fight you.
Then you win."

-Mahatma Gandhi

INTRODUCTION

What this book will do for you:

This book will help you open your third eye to the corruption within the courts and the proceedings that go overlooked because government officials use their position of power to undermine the system. There are many people out there who are defeated by everyday issues that seem too difficult to overcome. These struggles exhaust and lower themselves to levels of hopelessness, resentment, and failure.

I feel that it is heartbreaking that people let their problems, circumstances and difficulties stress them to the stage of no ambition, maturation, or determination. I had my problems. I have overcome some and as it is in life, continue to right the others. I have written this book to teach you that it is possible to overcome life's hardships, by applying your mindset to believe that victory can be achieved instead of believing that failure is written in stone.

By learning to cast negativity from the mind and refusing to become mentally subservient to such thoughts, faith and self-belief can help you rise above any obstacles that normally may conquer you. The purpose of this is a very direct exposure of how the author, Matthew Pugh, used his own vision, intellect, and faith to find the miscarriage of justice that was overlooked by the professional counsels that handle high profile cases in the mainstream courtroom. These same professional counsels never acknowledged that something was just not right with my case, based on the facts and evidence both presented and withheld.

The fact that there were numerous flaws in my trial should be enough to start a conversation. It is my hope that the shady, unjust tactics that go on in cases are brought to the light and a realization occurs which will show that prosecutors deal daily in deceptive tactics to win at all costs, and to swing what they deem as justice their own way.

How can I be so certain that the practice of these principals will produce such results? The solution is remarkably simple. A "wokeness" is happening to the people of our society and this "wokeness" is providing a look at the true workings of the court system and the prison industrial complex. A clear understanding is dawning of what the system does to the unlucky that are not in the grips of the system. That which has been discovered and understood, has made the people fed up!

Celebrity leaders such as Sunny Hostin, who has been a prosecutor and who has a clear inside understanding of the system has a better vantage point to recognize the unjust flaws of the system which can bring about a conversation. This conversation, hopefully, will bring to light the needed reforms to prevent corruption in the court system, and when it does happen, a swift remedy toward justice.

This book is a careful read of the techniques that I used to bring the corruption in my case to the light. The goal, is that anyone who reads this book, will be able to use the same formulas contained herein to set themselves free from the circumstances in their lives and from the personal bondage that may be preventing progress from taking control of the life being lived. This can be done by recognizing the leader that lives within and showing this by the way one moves. I speak with great knowledge which helped me become a person of great usefulness. It is my hope that the ones who have doubted themselves, will come into a new sense of well being and confidence.

It is my intention that these stories will show the reader that even with a sentence of sixty years, by corruption, I have stayed motivated in my quest for my leadership position and determination to prove the actual truth. I will not only show what transpired during my trial, but I will also give examples from my past which will include relationships, compassion, protection, and acceptance.

If there is just a mustard seed of faith inside of you, I urge you to just believe, for I am a true believer that God has bestowed His blessings upon me through this journey. I am stress-free, never worried, and full of spiritual happiness everyday that I wake up and witness a new day.

-Matthew Pugh

Motivational Song - *"Fight For You"*
H.E.R.

TABLE OF CONTENTS

PROLOGUE: ORCHARD STREET

My parents were two hard working citizens that took pride in their work, especially after relocating from North Carolina. My family has been blessed to have strong bonds and opportunities to gather at reunions every year together.

The complex that we lived in was built like a maze and was a half a block from Saint Raphael Hospital. In the 1960's, Malcom X, and some of the members of the Black Panther Party resided in this complex. There was a major standoff at this complex between the Panther Party and the police, which played out on the roof top.

During my childhood, when I was around the ages of seven through nine, I remember helping my father keep the complex clean on a regular basis. I learned how to sand and strip cabinets, wax, and sand floors, and how to lay carpet and tile. This was all so that the new tenants would have a nice place to move into. I remember watching the other kids play while I worked inside apartments or helped my father clean the complex. This could be anytime during the day or the night.

My parents had three children. I am the oldest, my brother and I are four years apart, and my sister and I are six years apart. When we were growing up, my siblings and I wanted for nothing because my parents provided and taught us responsibility and how to be independent with handling chores at a very young age. My Father and mother were deeply religious as they were brought up Baptist, and whenever I spent time down south with my grandparents, I could see where they both got it from.

My grandmother would always read scriptures from the Bible and would quote verses that would let me know that God protects His children, regardless of how bad a neighborhood that child comes from. I would be thinking on what my grandmother was saying as I picked cucumbers in the field that my grandfather owned. This was hard work and it taught me that hard work does pay well. My sacks were heavy and filled from my labor, which paid me very well.

Back in New Haven, my parents would have us go to Church on Sundays at this cozy little church. The music at this Church which helped the congregation celebrate was full of joyful praise, helped along by the sounds of the bass guitar, piano, drums, and a choir.

During my youth, I did not attend a public school. I went to a Catholic school, which provided me with a solid foundation for my academic studies. The problem that I ran into at this school, however, was the older students who would pick on me or my brother because of our last name. I can remember when I was in the fourth grade when I fought an eighth grader and won. This was the first time the lads ever saw someone in a lower grade win a fight over someone that was much older. This brought me a lot of respect from the other lads, and the girls admired what I did very much.

When my mother would drop us off at school, it was prohibited to cross the street to go to the store if you were already on school property. I love taking risks however, and candy from the store was my way of keeping the girls next to me and it also made me many friends.

The year was in the late seventies and early eighties. The atmosphere on Orchard Street was violent. There were numerous shootings, drugs, pimps, prostitutes, and a lot of money being made in the neighborhood. People were always in the driveways with their flashy cars, or they were handling a drug sale somewhere. Others had conversations on their porch or were in the park.

I remember hearing the block parties getting louder and I wanted to be down in the streets so badly, but I just took it all in from my second-floor window. I could see people moving to the sounds of L.L. Cool J, Biz Markie, Slick Rick, KRS 1, Rakim, Kool G. Rap, Big Daddy Kane, ring my bells and juicy. The DJ that was doing his thing was related to L.L. Cool J. His name was Michael Smith. He lived next to my family, and everyone thought he was going to be L.L's DJ, because he was already doing gigs in New York City.

My father would normally play gospel music from Shirley Caesar, The might Clouds of Joy, Yolanda Adams, and others. The sound of Tom Joyner broadcast on 94.3 would also be heard through the apartment. I was getting the best of both music worlds all of the time.

I remember the times when I wanted to play with the lads outside but instead, I had to help my father keep the complex clean and tidy. I would sneak out to get my play time from the visions of the lads playing basketball with milk crates, swinging on monkey bars, and playing with colorful marbles at Kensington St. Park.

One day, I had to chase down this big marble in the K Street park and I slid in the grass. As I was getting up, I noticed there was blood dripping down my arm. A broken piece of glass had ripped my arm open. I ran home and treated the wound with alcohol and peroxide. I treated myself instead of going to the hospital to get stitched up. I am left with a long scar down my arm that always reminds me of my childhood.

The complex that I lived in had this big white concrete wall that I loved climbing. Upon reaching the top, I felt like I was on the top of the world. My parents put me into track because they noticed my speed as I ran to the corner store called Boomers, which was on Orchard and Edgewood Avenue. I loved racing my brother to the store when we were sent to purchase food for our parents. While we were there, I would get penny candies for my siblings and I and then it was back to racing to the apartment.

I received many trophies and medals for my speed. I was coached by Mr. Barber at Bowen Field, which is located behind Hillhouse High School in New Haven, Connecticut. Track and field and Football were the sports that I loved. My school never had a Football team, so I would play in the Hood in either K-Street or Dwight Park. My speed enabled me to never be tacked. My agility would let me skate right past people. I wonder if my parents really knew how gifted I was at football. If they did, I could have gone places and had a different life.

My parents always prepared delicious home cooked meals and I learned quickly at an early age how to prepare breakfast for them. They taught me how to be independent and crafty as well. There was a time when my parents put my skills to the test. They had me prepare breakfast for them. I put it together with the help of my brother and sister. To-gether, we set the table and poured the orange juice and brough the meal upstairs to my parents' bedroom. This was the first time that I knew I could cook because the plates came back empty. By being attentive to my parents while they cooked, the payoff has blessed me with this gift that continues to benefit me to this day.

As I became older, things began to change for me. A lad would al-ways try to come into my complex, and I was not feeling that...so I beat him up. One day, however, He got tired of the beatings, and he monkey flipped me on K-street and we became best friends. I never knew he was curious about my life and family. At the same time, he did not know that I was curious about the life that he lived on the streets. He wore flashy clothing and the latest sneakers. I introduced him to my family, and he wanted to run track with me. As all of this was going on, I wanted to know more about how he got all that money and how he got to be out at all times during the day and the night.

My world went from cleaning up the complex and renovating apartments to running away from home and getting a taste of that street life. I remember my first-time selling drugs. It was red bags of powder that cost $25 a bag. I would get a bundle, take $100 and get back $400. One day, the block was booming, and the other dealers went to a concert at the New Haven Coliseum. I stayed back with my friend to hustle and to my surprise, made $2000 in a half an hour.

I was hooked and addicted to selling drugs at that moment. You could not tell me anything! I said to myself, "I can make this much in this little time, I am going to be rich!" This is when the girls started to come around, doing what teenagers do. I had at this time enough mastery within myself to meet an independent and beautiful woman who was six years older than me. From her, I was able to learn many different responsibilities that came with life.

With the first $2,000 I made, I went and had a Bally suit tailored by a fashion designer named Unique. He laced this black and red outfit and I could see now why all the drug dealers in the Hood took their clothes to him. I made sure that I brough some suede black and red Bally shoes to complete the outfit. I climbed up that wall in my complex and thought about the song by Nas, "If I Ruled The World." I took a picture of this glorious moment.

Orchard street was my stomping ground that led me to learn the drug trade at an early age. My mentors were big time pushers that I picked up jewels from. From mastering these lessons, I began to create my own empire on a unique block that looked like the suburbs. This was Dwight street and in Fair Haven, a street called Popular.

During my experience with the street life and the money that I used to make so I could survive on my own, I had to come up with a place to become stable instead of living the way that I was. I was moving from house to house with friends, girls, or a hotel room that friends and I would rent for a week.

There was that one beautiful older lady that most of the dealers on K street were trying to talk to and get with. I decided to build a relationship with her. This at the time seemed like the best move to me because she taught me how to drive my first standard car which was a Saab 900. After that, I was hooked on standard cars. From downshifting to burning out on the road and speeding off! I never bought another automatic car after my first, which was a Volkswagen Jetta. This older woman was a certified nursing assistant (or C.N.A), and she taught me how to save money, pay bills, and budget.

As I began to hustle in the early 90's while I was with this woman, selling powder was my thing. I had good quality cocaine that had the customers coming back to me. One day, out of all days, a dealer gave me some weed to sell. I gave him a look as if to say, "come on man! You know I sell powder," but he was trying to start weed on the block, so I took the weed. A half hour after he gave me the weed, I was busted by the drug narcotic task force in the apartment that I shared with this older woman.

I thanked God that the police did not find the cocaine that I had stashed under the stairs. All they found was 70-100 bags of weed. The funny thing about this is that I had to do my first bid for weed instead of cocaine possession. This was a blessing, as I could have received a harsher sentence. I was sent to a Connecticut youth facility and had to do a year, but with a 10% reduction of the sentence, I only ended up serving a month.

I was put on parole and probation, and had a bracelet placed on me that monitored my movements. The system wanted to link the device to my father's apartment, but I did not want to go back to his home due to my addicted lifestyle. I ended up cutting the bracelet off and ended up on the run for six to seven years. I was still in a relationship with this older lady.

Now this older lady had to move due to the raid on her apartment on K street. I took responsibility because it was my duty as a man to step up because she would not have been getting evicted if it was not for my drug activity. I scraped up the security deposit and the first months rent for a new place on Howe street across from the pizza house which still makes delicious pizza to this day.

This is where I came across a banging connection. They were two older dealers from New York City that pushed weight off to Amsterdam, 157, and Broadway. They supplied me with top notch cocaine that I sold around my neighborhood for $25. From doing this, I was flipping my money over the $5 sales that they were making. I was finally introduced to a Dominican connection on the block in New York City. I would buy weight from them in powdered form, and I would have a lady whom I'll call Blondie, who would cook it up in a coffee pot.

The quality was so good that when I would buy 200 grams, the cocaine would jump back to over an ounce once it was cooked up. This gave me an even greater profit from the streets. My hustling mentality in the streets ended up pushing me away from the older woman that I had a relationship with because I did not want to settle down. I was making a lot of money and I was living a fast life with different beautiful women and partying it up with my boys.

This is how I was introduced to my second cousin, Gus. Gus will be discussed later in this book, and I will explain how our relationship was built through protection and loyalty.

The street life was so good to me in the early 90's and I remember going through many women. There was always one woman who stuck out however, and her name was Tasha. Tasha was originally from Maryland. She was exquisite and had the features of a model with big bright glossy emerald eyes. She stood between 5'7 and 5'8 to my 5'5 but the height difference did not matter to us because we were both caught up in the moment when we began to build with each other.

I was introduced to her through my second Cousin Gus's girlfriend, who at the time was a Columbian named Carmen. Tasha stayed with Carmen at this time because she did not have anywhere else to go after having moved from Maryland in order to pursue her modeling as well as her hairstyling skills.

Tasha had become caught up in a difficult relationship with a Jamaican guy from Bridgeport. She had wanted out of the relationship because of his possessive and controlling behavior. Due to this, I suggested to Tasha that she come and stay with me so that she could get away from this complex relationship. I wanted her to start new without any worries or problems. I would make sure that he could not find her, and I would take care of her. She agreed because she was feeling me, and I was building with her every time I was at Carmen's house with Gus.

I stepped up to the plate and began a new relationship with Tasha. She was the woman that I was going to marry, but there was just one thing that made me second guess my commitment to her. This was the street life. I was addicted to this life as if it were a drug and I knew deep down inside that I would not be able to be loyal as long as I stayed in the streets. She was my best friend, my ride or die chick! We did everything together including traveling to the city, shopping in Harlem and Queens, even bouncing down to Maryland, to her town to visit her family.

Tasha was so thorough at driving that I felt comfortable and safe with her anytime she was behind the wheel. She was the first woman that I went out of my way to purchase a car for. I purchased her something right off of the showroom floor of the dealership on Whalley Avenue. It was a black Coupe with chrome five-star rims, and it was very fast. Tasha knew how to drive a standard as well, so it was even more perfect that I did not have to teach her how to.

In New Haven, everyone knew about us and supported our relationship to the fullest. The love that was between us was seen by everyone. I remember going to the mall and paying $5,000 for a marquise cut diamond ring that had diamonds uniquely set on the side. The asking price was $6,500 but I was able to talk the jeweler down and I walked out with this prestigious rock which I intended to give to Tasha. Even with the ring and the happiness however, the life in the streets was very tempting and women pursued me to make me their own.

I remember coping my red GT Probe with 18-inch gold and chrome rimes. It was a standard of course, and I also coped my black 300 ZX Twin Turbo Nissan with T-Tops. You could not tell me nothing! I would get the cars detailed in the Hood and as soon as they were done, I would do donuts in the road and whip out down the street with music blasting and my car sparkling.

I thought Tasha and I would last, but I was tempted by one of my workers. I had a group of girls that sold cocaine and this one was eager to make money. She was on point, which caught my interest. She would keep the girls and money in order, but it was her loyalty that attracted me the most. Knowing that I was in a relationship was not a barrier in her eyes. She aimed, she shot, and she captured.

I fell for Audrey. There was just something incredibly special about her. Her sign was a Libra, just like my mother and I loved the way she handled herself. I end up getting her pregnant, and this was before I had to go and do a bid for assaulting a guy that disrespected me. I went in for six and a half years. Before that started, I had the chance to get to the hospital and record MY Latin cherub being delivered. This was a beautiful moment. I never had a weak stomach for something as glorious as bringing life into the world. I appreciate and I am incredibly grateful to have experienced that moment. My daughter was born in January 1998, and I had to leave to do a bid in early February 1998.

The street life of my youth made me who I am today, and why I can say, most of this would leave the average person speechless. A song from Nas, "had my vision and brainstorming unique ideas of hustling mentality will guarantee to bring me longevity and prosperity towards the future." I say to anyone that has been through anything similar, to use your mind to take you where you need to go in life. Learn from mistakes and stop repeating generational issues that keep you down and prevent you from your own greatness!

My greatness has always been within me since my childhood and although I dropped out of high school, my success to see the real design of my life is now starting to appear to the world. So, stay tuned, for the gem that will keep shining wherever I go!

Motivational Song - *"Rather You than Me"*
Rick Ross/Dej Loaf
"Maybach Music V"

If communication had been better between attorney and client, the gas station could have been a material witness that would have proved detective Arthur Higgens committed perjury on the stand concerning his watching of the video at the specific times. This could have happened by simply calling the attendant to the stand, the truth about the watching of the tape would have come out which would have showed that the surveillance system was not turned on at the time in question. Doubt would have been cast upon the detective's testimony and the overall investigation.

The frustration that I felt as the video played was evident and seeing this detective testify falsely made me kick my attorney under the table and inform him that the testimony which was being given was in fact, false. If this defense attorney had not thought about the attendant's testimony as irrelevant, huge points would have been scored for my defense and with the jury. This is just the start of not being on the same page as to his representation of my defense.

This was the third strike thus far. First, the statue of limitations on the burglary charge. Second, allowing a juror to stay on the panel that said that she knew the victim's cousin, "Brenda" who worked with her in Southbury, Connecticut. Third, the video surveillance from the Hess gas station which had never been turned on. I thought to myself that this may be the nail in the coffin.

With the blinding of the Judge, Jury, and attorney, as to this evidence, I knew that this game was not being played fair. As the loopholes for freedom started to slip away, so did my trust for my trial attorney. Any one of those incidents could have been a chance to win the jury over but they were lost. I stayed focused, and now it is paying off in further proceedings. I want you to pay close attention to the next chapter as I show you just how important it was for me to pick up on this false, misleading testimony.

Try and see if you can spot the loopholes that went over all the heads at the trial include the judge, the jury, trial attorneys and even the innocent assistant Amy Bepko who was the only person that knew that perjury was being committed by the state's attorney Lawlar and Detective Huggins. I'll get to you, Amy Bepko, in another chapter, I just wanted you to know how corrupt your boss was with handling this case. You were clueless and I could see this in your eyes.

That is alright however, because now it is exposed, and you can regret not putting more effort into this case while you were working at the state attorney's office. I had the hope that you would realize that your boss and the Milford Police were setting me up. This case was not managed with integrity, honesty, or fairness. Ms. Bepko, I believe that you were kept in the dark, but that does not excuse you from using your own intellect, knowledge, and understanding of this case. You were not the only one who was taken advantage of by the state. Sunny Hostin from the view has also reported on my case, without knowing all the facts concerning this case.

We live in strange times, where wrongful convictions seem to be normal and police brutality headlines clog the news feeds. I am just an average citizen that was tried and convicted wrongfully due to a need to close a cold case in which the state employed malicious and nefarious tactics that infected this case. This resulted in the wrongful conviction I am now serving time for.

CHAPTER 1

BIASED JUROR

The defendant rights of Due Process of Law, the Fifth Amendment to the U.S. Constitution provides, in part, that a person can not be deprived of life, liberty or property without Due Process of law. This Due Process clause is the basis for many of the rights afforded to criminal defendants and procedures followed in criminal courts.

Procedural Due Process means that before a criminal defendant can be punished, they must be given a legitimate opportunity to contest the chargers against them. For example, Matthew Pugh is entitled to be put on notice of the charges long enough before trial to have a chance to prepare a defense and be entitled to be tried by a fair and impartial Judge and jury.

In the case of the State of Connecticut v. Matthew Pugh, the defendant was never afforded his right to a fair jury, as a juror was placed on the jury even after the Court and attorneys found out that this juror knew the alleged victim's cousin, "Brenda," in Southbury, Connecticut. It is my belief that from the beginning, my jury selection was set up by Judge Denise Markle, prosecutor Kevin Lawlar and attorney Paul Carty. My belief is born from the fact that in 2012, I was charged with first degree murder and first-degree burglary.

This first-degree burglary charge had passed the Statue of Limitations, due to this murder on May 19, 2006, and being charged on September 5, 2012. That is six years past the incident of the murder, and no one acknowledged the five-year limitation on prosecution when the pre-trial proceedings were happening. I did not know too much about the law at the time, but yet I questioned myself about the statue of limitation rule.

If I had questions about the legality of the limitation, should the professionals also have easily noticed this?

CHAPTER 2

INEFFECTIVE ASSISTANCE OF COUNSEL

I still remember the day that Attorney Paul Carty visited me at the now closed Northern Correctional institution after having the case from the end of 2012. This attorney was appointed to represent me Pro Bono counsel. Northern Correction Institution is a maze of protective plastic, and one cannot move through this prison without being seen.

While I was at recreation in the red jumper that was issued to me, my conversation with my associates was cut short when the loudspeaker announced my name. I looked up and could see that attorney Paul Carty was standing on the top level of this protective glass rubix cube. Some-one shouted, "Hey Breed, is that your lawyer? He looks like a gangster with his black shades on." My question was, why did it take this attorney so long to visit me?

Finally, I was face to face with this attorney, and he tells me that we are about to go to trial, and we need to begin picking jurors at the start of 2015. As Carty continued to speak, he came to the part where he wanted to file a speedy trial due to the fact that there was no DNA, eyewitnesses, forensics, or other evidence connecting me to the murder, but due to some court issues it would have to wait until 2015.

I had some of my own questions, so I asked Carty if he had investigated the gas station attendant at the Hess station on Dixwell Avenue. His response was that it was not relevant. I strongly felt that it was relevant because this was the first place that I stopped on May 19, 2006, to get gas around 9am, for my 4-door green Acura. Follow along readers and see if you can connect the dots to the loopholes and mistakes of this incompetent lawyer in defending me against these corrupt officers.

It is May 22, 2006, 3 days after the murder and I am the person of interest in this murder investigation. I vividly remember going to the Hess gas station in the mid-morning with my baby's mother, Charise Trotman's gold expedition to get gas. The attendant was a black man, who came to the side door to inform me that two Milford Police officers came to question him with my photo. He then stated that he thought he was going to be fired because he did not have the video recording turned on during his shift.

It did not register in my mind to think that this one day may be a crucial part of proving my innocence years later after being charged with 1st degree murder and burglary on September 5, 2012. There are moments in life that keep you aware of mistakes involving procedures to your circumstances and this is one of those moments. Something was not adding up with the investigation.

Transcript: February 19, 2015

Prosecutor: Q. Now also, without stating what was said, were you also requested to verify whether or not the defendant had been to the Hess gas station in Hamden on the day May 19, 2006?

Arthur Huggins: A. Yes.

Q. And do you recall going to the station?

A. Yes, I do.

Q. Alright. If you could just explain to the ladies and gentlemen of the jury what happened? I believe you went there twice, correct?

A. Yes, we did.

Q. Okay. If you could just explain to the ladies and gentlemen of the jury how that went.

A. Sure. One of the things that came up during the investigation and the interview was that he was—Mr. Pugh—was at the Hess gas station there during the day, earlier in the day. So, we went there in an effort to locate—everyone has surveillance tapes, so we wanted to go in there and look at their tapes to see in fact if he was there or wasn't there. We went in and talked to the store owner, and they had to pull things up on the videos. When they started showing them, we said, you this is the gentleman we are looking for, and it was Mr. Pugh. We had a photo of him. He said, "Oh, he sells sneakers." So, we started going through the times and at 14:10, that is ten after 2:00, we located Mr. Pugh going up to the cashier and paying at the store front. It was later in the afternoon.

Q. Showing you what's been marked as state's exhibit 4 as a full exhibit. Does that hat look similar to the one you observed in the video?

A. Yes. That's—yes.

Q. and did you earlier look again at the surveillance video that you took—that you seized from Hess gas station on that day?

A. Yes, I did.

Q. And were you again able to locate at 2:10, the person who you identified, based on the photograph and the dress, as the defendant?

A. Yes, I was.

Q. And does it fairly and accurately reflect the video that you observed, both at the Hess gas station and then brought back to the police station after you watched the video?

A. Yes, it is.

Whereupon state's exhibit 62 was marked as a full exhibit.

Lawlar: If I may, your Honor, I would ask that this be played for the jury at this time.

Court: Alright.

Lawlar: While that is being cued up, I have another question for you. How long of a time frame did you watch at the Hess gas station that day? Like, what was the time that you start—you know as far as the video that you were watching, what time did it start and what time did it end?

A. We started at 9:00 and we kind of fast forwarded and as people came into views, we would play and look at it just to confirm whether or not, and then just keep continuing. I believe it was until probably about 1:00 in the afternoon we had looked at it then, you know at the time. They couldn't get it off of the—they couldn't download it onto a disk for us and at that time we added more time to it.

Q. Okay. So, for the first time from 9:00 to 11:00, were you able to match anyone who matched the defendant's description?

A. No, we were not.

Q. And the second time were you able to—when you went further in the day, were you able to find somebody?

A. Yes.

Q. And what is the time that you observed on the video that the jury is about to see?

A. 14:10 hours.

Q. And 14:10, for these folks no in the miliary?

A. 2:10

Q. 2:10 in the afternoon?

A. Yes.

Lawlar: Yes, your honor. The state would ask that the state's exhibit 62, which was marked as a full exhibit, be played for the jury.

Court: Alright.

Direct examination by Attorney Lawlar Continued...

Q. Okay. This is upside down, correct? What time does it state?

A. It just went away.

Q. 2006

Lawlar: Do it again. If you freeze it, it goes off again?

Q. And what time is this, 2006?

A. It's 14:10

A: Right in the middle.

Q. Okay. Is that the individual there that you recognize based on the clothing?

A. Upside down, yes, it is.

Q. Okay. So, I'd ask that this be inverted. There we go, and again, that was at what time?

A. That was at 14:10.

Q. Nothing further.

If you have followed the Court's demonstration of trying to play a video recording of me going to get gas at the Hess gas station at 9am and 2:10

pm, but the state was only able to show me on the video at 2:10pm and not 9am. This is because Milford Police as well as the prosecutor Kevin Lawlar, knew that they could not show me at 9am at the Hess gas station due to the fact that the Hess gas station attendant on May 19, 2006, did not turn on the video surveillance during his shift.

Even though I did go to the Hess gas station at 9am, Arthur Huggins of the Milford Police department lied about watching the video from 9am to 1pm, and no individuals fitting my description was ever known at that time. The police and the prosecutor knew what they were doing. I do not believe that the Judge, jury, or my trial attorney knew of what these governmental officials were doing in this court of law.

They never showed any individuals from the time of 9am to 1pm to prove that I was not telling the truth. The reason that they could not show any individual was because they never watched a video of that time frame. This is perjury. Committed to fool the jury, Judge, and my counsel. The state claimed that the video was freezing up. If the Judge, jury, and my counsel learned the truth, the lies would have been uncovered, which would have exposed the liars that they are.

This is a single example of the importance of me asking my then attorney, Paul Carty, about the video and reveals his failure to understand the relevance to the matter. The gas station attendant should have been investigated. This would have proven that there were lies being told and that there was no surveillance footage. It was never turned on by this attendant who was worried about the possibility of being fired for this mistake.

I was never seen on the video at 9am , but the police testified that they watched the video from 9am until 2pm. Who ever pulled into the Hess gas station after the attendant failed to activate the recording system was not seen until the attendant's shift was over. The next shifts attendant did turn the system on, capturing me on video at 2:10pm.

Chapter 3

False Misleading Testimony

Statement of the issue:

Whether the witness for the prosecutor testified to false misleading testimony at trial describing defendant's shoe in violation of covering up favorable and material evidence found at the crime scene.

On Friday May 19, 2006, Detective Arthur Huggins received a call to assist the head detective that was at the scene of the crime. Huggins met with detective Ron and started going over the actual incident. The investigation started at this point.

Detective Huggins was asked by Prosecutor Kevin Lawlar on cross examination, who was in charge at that point based on the orders that were given at that time. Huggins stated that Sargent Youd was there, Detective Ron was there, and Detective Ron was also his lead.

Huggins was asked, "At that point, were you given any particular tasks to handle by a lead at the crime scene?" Huggin's response was that he was. Detective Huggins and Ron were instructed to follow up on the defendant Matthew Pugh as a person of interest and find out where the defendant was on the same day, May 19, 2006, as well as who he was with and so on and so forth.

Detective Huggins and Ron, through their investigation of the evening of May 19, 2006, located Matthew Pugh at Papa John's through a conversation with Charise Trotman at 98 North Street in Hamden Connecticut. Ms. Trotman allowed the detectives into her home and answered all of their questions pertaining to Matthew Pugh. Ms. Trotman was asked if Matthew Pugh had changed clothes. She indicated that yes, he had changed clothes and that the clothing he had changed out of was on the bed.

There were a pair of black pants and gray sweatpants. The detectives just glanced at the clothes without picking them up or examining them and said O.K. Ms. Trotman indicated to the detectives that after removing the clothing that was left on the bed, Matthew Pugh put on his Papa John's uniform and left for work. (I also was wearing red and white sneakers).

Once the detectives learned that I may be at the Papa John's on Whalley Avenue in New Haven Connecticut, they proceed to the establishment to make it known that they were officers and they wanted to speak to me. The detectives did not want to talk in the restaurant, so we all proceeded to go outside. They informed that Alexandra Ducsay was deceased. The detectives then made it known that they did not want to continue their investigation in the middle of the parking lot and asked me if I would come down to headquarters. I said sure.

They then asked me if they could look at my sneakers. Detective Huggins wanted to see the color, the pattern, and also to take down a description of them. Huggins looked at my clothing and stated that he was looking for any blood that could be visible to the naked eye but stated that he could not see any. Huggins noted that my sneakers were black and white, and that sole had a pyramid type of design but did not see anything on them.

To my readers, have you discovered the loophole yet? Why would Detective Huggins describe a shoe with a pyramid type design when I was wearing New Balance sneakers and no New Balance sneaker has this type of design on the sole? Detectives Huggins and Ron were both given the particular task from the lead detective at the crime scene at 3 Boothbay street in Milford Connecticut, which was to check Matthew Pugh's sneaker soles for a pyramid type design, to attempt to match it to the one left at the crime scene in the blood.

The States theory was that I wore a body suit, which was alleged by own cousin, Anthony Pugh, to explain why there was no DNA evidence found at the crime scene. The State withheld favorable and material evidence by failing to mention to the jury or turn over to my counsel in discovery that there was a bloody pyramid type shoe prints left in the blood throughout the crime scene. This evidence and strange testimony clearly point to my innocence. The State's attorney, Kevin Lawlar, knew about this evidence. In his own words, from the May 11 transcript, he describes vividly the crime scene as he visited it on May 19, 2006.

Quote: This was to put it mildly, a savage attack. I think as testimony by some officers at the scene, some of whom are here today, said on those days that this was one of the worst crime scenes that they have ever seen or could imagine, and that is for me too.

You know it is almost nine years to the day now and I as well walked down those steps and saw this young woman basically beaten beyond recognition.

This is proof that the prosecutor, Kevin Lawlar, was at the crime scene and conducted the investigation with the detectives, Chief of Police, and the State Police, and all were involved with the handling of evidence on May 19, 2006. Why then, I ask, was there not any mention of this favorable evidence of these bloody shoe prints with a pyramid type of design in the discovery or introduced at my trial?

State of Connecticut Dept. of Public Safety Narrative Report DPS-302-C (Revised 04/'03)	REPORT TYPE:	ATTACHMENTS:	DPS INCIDENT NUMBER:
	[X] INITIAL CONTINUATION [ ] SUPPLEMENTARY [ ] RE-OPEN [X] ASSIST [ ] CLOSING	[ ] STATEMENTS [ ] PHOTOGRAPHS [ ] SKETCH MAP [ ] EVIDENCE [ ] TELETYPE [X] OTHER	DPS06-022551 Page 12 of 16

was used. Evidentiary items numbered SP-10 through SP-14 consisted of sections of the basement carpeting that constituted the path from the stairwell to the bedroom in the southwest corner of the basement. The carpeting showed signs of some possible blood like drops in the south room, leading to the bedroom. The sections of carpeting were seized as they may be reviewed by the Forensic Laboratory and perhaps trace evidence from the suspect, or a shoe or foot impression may be obtained that may belong to a suspect. Evidentiary item number SP-15 was a white t-shirt found on the bed in the basement. This shirt was very damp and appeared to have red, blood like staining on it. Also seized were items numbered SP-16 through SP-18, consisted of pieces of a baseboard heating cover along the north wall in the basement. The area closest to the stairs appeared to have significant amounts of what was believed to be blood on them. They further had an area of significant transfer and a possible swipe mark. Evidentiary items numbered SP-19 through SP-22 consisted of swabbings of red, blood like staining in various areas of the residence. Of note is item SP-19, which was a swabbing obtained from the interior side of the half wall at the bottom of the stairwell. The blood like drops appeared to be dropping straight down and did not appear to be "spatter". As such, this blood could show a prior injury to the deceased before reaching the downstairs area, or it could be blood from a suspect who obtained an injury during the attack. Evidentiary item number SP-23 and SP-24 consisted of a door knob and tablecloth in the hallway atop the basement stairwell that appeared to have blood like stains on them. Evidentiary items numbered SP-25 through SP-27 consisted of swabbings of the blood areas identified in the first floor bathroom. It is unknown if this blood belongs to the deceased, or her attacker. Evidentiary item number SP-28 consisted of the latent prints (LP#1-LP#7) taken from the interior of the residence, and evidentiary item number SP-29 was a control sample of a distilled water swabbing.

At the conclusion of scene processing, all items were turned over to Detective Gall of the Milford Police Department Identification Unit. This was done at approximately 0730 hours. Detective Gall and I discussed each item of evidence and physically located each item so that all items were turned over together.

It should be noted that subsequent scene processing on Wednesday, May 24, 2006 that was requested by Milford Police Detectives, resulted in an eighth latent print being found (LP#8) and it being collected under evidentiary item number SP-30. This was also turned over to Detective Gall and was done so at approximately 1320 hours.

Action Taken: On Friday, May 19, 2006 at approximately 1900 hours members of the Connecticut State Police Central District Major Crime Squad were requested to respond to the Milford Police Department to assist in processing a murder scene. Investigators arrived at the Police Department at approximately 2120 hours, each driving their assigned departmental vehicle, with the exception of Detective Guida who had driven the unit's crime van. Upon everyone's arrival, investigators were given a brief synopsis, which follows, of the events that lead to the request for assistance.

CASE STATUS:		TYPE OF EXCEPTIONAL CLEARANCE:	
[X] 1-ACTIVE [ ] 2-CLEARED ARREST [ ] 3-SUSPENDED	[ ] 4-EXCEPTIONAL CLEARANCE [ ] 6-NO CRIMINAL ASPECT [ ] F-FUGITIVE	[ ] A-OFFENDER DECEASED [ ] B-PROSECUTION DENIED [ ] C-EXTRADITION DENIED	[ ] D-VICTIM UNCOOPERATIVE [ ] E-JUVENILE-NO CUSTODY

THE UNDERSIGNED, AN INVESTIGATOR DULY SWORN, DEPOSES AND SAYS THAT; I AM THE WRITER OF THE ATTACHED POLICE REPORT PERTAINING TO THIS INCIDENT NUMBER. THAT THE INFORMATION CONTAINED THEREIN WAS SECURED AS A RESULT OF (1) MY PERSONAL OBSERVATIONS & KNOWLEDGE; OR (2) INFORMATION RELAYED TO ME BY OTHER MEMBERS OF MY POLICE DEPARTMENT OR OF ANOTHER POLICE DEPARTMENT; OR (3) INFORMATION SECURED BY MYSELF OR ANOTHER MEMBER OF A POLICE DEPARTMENT FROM THE PERSONS NAMED OR IDENTIFIED THEREIN, AS INDICATED IN THE ATTACHED REPORT. THAT THE REPORT IS AN ACCURATE STATEMENT OF THE INFORMATION SO RECEIVED BY ME.

INVESTIGATOR SIGNATURE	INVESTIGATOR I.D.	REPORT DATE	SUPERVISOR SIGNATURE	SUPERVISOR I.D.	APPROVAL DATE
DET. JAMES CANON JR.	1107	5/30/06	SGT. PAUL HEON	218	6-1-2006

State of Connecticut Dept. of Public Safety Narrative Report	REPORT TYPE:	ATTACHMENTS:	DPS INCIDENT NUMBER:
	X INITIAL CONTINUATION SUPPLEMENTARY RE-OPEN X ASSIST CLOSING	STATEMENTS PHOTOGRAPHS SKETCH MAP EVIDENCE TELETYPE X OTHER	DPS06-022551
DPS-302-C (Revised 04/'03)			Page 14 of 16

During the course of removing the exterior clothing of the deceased, two pieces of evidentiary value were discovered under the left side of the head. Attached to the left cheek of the deceased was a piece of black colored tape, approximately 1 ½" inches in width. The tape was documented appropriately and subsequently removed and seized. A look at the deceased's face revealed that there was a void of blood and biological material beneath where the tape had been. This leads to the conclusion that the tape may have been placed there prior to the injuries. Also, found beneath the head of the deceased was a knife blade. The blade had no distinguishing features, other than the fact that there was no handle. It appeared to be a common kitchen style knife, but a check of the residence revealed no such similar knives.

The deceased was then removed from the scene at approximately 0150 hours on Saturday, May 20, 2006 by members of the Office of the Chief Medical Examiner.

Investigators then began to locate, mark and document items of evidence value. Investigators marked several areas of carpeting from the stairwell to the deceased, and from the deceased to the basement bedroom. These areas were cut out in five sections and packaged accordingly. The carpeting was seized on the presumption that the scene was very brutal and bloody, and as such the suspect would have had a significant amount of transferred blood on their person. With the possibility of a blood trail leading to the back bedroom, there is a chance that the laboratory may be able to identify a foot impression or other trace evidence on the carpeting.

It should be noted that the Milford Police Department did seize the desktop computer from the dining room, as well as the laptop computer in the eastern bedroom atop the second floor stairwell, at approximately 0010 hours on May 20, 2006.

Investigators continued to process the residence throughout the night and into the morning hours for items of evidentiary value. Each time an item was located, it was marked accordingly and documented through the audio/video recording and 35mm and digital photography.

After collecting items of evidentiary value, investigators then attempted to obtain latent prints inside the residence, in particular the areas around where the deceased was located. Investigators further used Ortho-tolidine, a chemical reagent for identifying blood, in an attempt to locate bloody prints or indications of a disturbance in the crime scene. Through the use of Ortho-tolidine, investigators learned that there was blood in the first floor bathroom, but there was nothing found that would assist in identification of a suspect.

At the conclusion of processing the interior of the residence for evidentiary items, investigators conducted a search of the fenced in back yard. The search found nothing of evidentiary value.

CASE STATUS:		TYPE OF EXCEPTIONAL CLEARANCE:	
X 1-ACTIVE	4-EXCEPTIONAL CLEARANCE	A-OFFENDER DECEASED	D-VICTIM UNCOOPERATIVE
2-CLEARED ARREST	6-NO CRIMINAL ASPECT	B-PROSECUTION DENIED	E-JUVENILE-NO CUSTODY
3-SUSPENDED	F-FUGITIVE	C-EXTRADITION DENIED	

THE UNDERSIGNED, AN INVESTIGATOR DULY SWORN, DEPOSES AND SAYS THAT: I AM THE WRITER OF THE ATTACHED POLICE REPORT PERTAINING TO THIS INCIDENT NUMBER. THAT THE INFORMATION CONTAINED THEREIN WAS SECURED AS A RESULT OF (1) MY PERSONAL OBSERVATIONS & KNOWLEDGE; OR (2) INFORMATION RELAYED TO ME BY OTHER MEMBERS OF MY POLICE DEPARTMENT OR OF ANOTHER POLICE DEPARTMENT; OR (3) INFORMATION SECURED BY MYSELF OR ANOTHER MEMBER OF A POLICE DEPARTMENT FROM THE PERSONS NAMED OR IDENTIFIED THEREIN, AS INDICATED IN THE ATTACHED REPORT. THAT THE REPORT IS AN ACCURATE STATEMENT OF THE INFORMATION SO RECEIVED BY ME.

INVESTIGATOR SIGNATURE	INVESTIGATOR I.D.	REPORT DATE	SUPERVISOR SIGNATURE	SUPERVISOR I.D.	APPROVAL DATE
DET. JAMES CANON JR.	1107	5/30/06	SGT. PAUL HEON	218	6-1-206

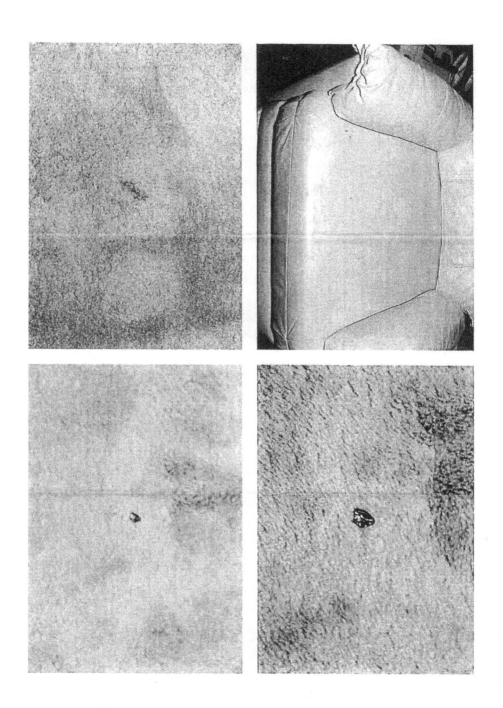

The corruption is just starting to become exposed. The next chapter will explain how these corrupt police officers and prosecutor managed this investigation and how corruption to blind unknowing members that were on the same team to obtain their desired conviction.

Chapter 4

Corrupt Police Department and Prosecutor but Innocent Assistant

Whether the Milford police and the prosecutor withheld favorable evidence from the crime scene, committing legal error for not introducing a bloody shoe print with a pyramid type design and not turning over this evidence in discovery, which violated the defendant's Constitutional rights.

Transcript February 10, 2015, William Cable

On Friday, May 19, 2006, Lieutenant Cable arrived at 3 Boothway Street, Milford Connecticut 06460 to assist Officer Frith with an investigation that included a homicide. While Frith continued to talk to Linda Ducsay outside the house at the front door, Lieutenant Cable was the first to discover Alexandra Ducsay born December 9, 1979, lying motionless on the floor.

He stated there was a lot of blood and what he thought was brain matter next to the deceased's head. Cable checked to see if the chest of the deceased was rising and falling, indicating a sign of breathing or life. There was neither. Cable, a trained officer, noticed other things, such as blood splatter. The splatter could be seen going in different directions and was found in different areas. Not only in the doorway, describing the bottom of the stairway, but none in that area, which means that there was more than one thing that caused the blood splatter because it was in different locations and in different directions.

Lieutenant Cable described the victim's wounds to the head as severe, massive, and probably the worst that he had ever seen. He stated that he did not see any type of weapon or instrument near the victim that would have caused that trauma. He described his nerves as slightly tense and stated that he was fearful about what he would find around the corner. He stated that there was blood all over the place and that it was pretty overwhelming. No one was found in the basement and Frith was advised that the party was deceased which made the area a crime scene.

Lieutenant Cable stated, "This is standard procedure, you don't want to compromise the integrity of the scene," he then stated, "You leave the deceased there and you make sure you know any type of proper documentation or evidence collection can be conducted." Lieutenant Cable stayed in the basement until the firefighters came down to the crime scene to verify that the party was officially deceased, and to make sure that no one came down, besides them.

Lieutenant Cable started a log which was kept on scene. Lieutenant Cable stated that they started to write down who came into the area, who left, what time they got there and what time they left at. He stated that this was standard procedure. Lieutenant Cable stated that he was in the residence for a half an hour or short period of time with the logbook before he handed the log book over to another officer.

Detective Frank Gall was the lead investigator at the crime scene for the Milford Police Department. On May 19, 2006, he helped the state police major crime unit investigate the crime scene, including all evidence near the victim and the murder. I want you to pay close attention to how Detective Gall was able to investigate the crime scene five hours before the state police arrived on the scene.

Transcript February 19, 2015
Detective Frank Gall, 430 Boston Post Rd. Milford Connecticut, 06460

On Friday, May 19, 2006, Gall received a call at home to come back to work for a possible homicide. Gall returned to work. On arrival, he went straight to his office and started to secure equipment that he might need. Gall was assisted by Detective Reardon because his current partner, Sergeant Carney, was off for the day. Gall and Reardon arrived at 3 Boothbay Street, Milford Connecticut 06460, and met with Chief Melo and Inspector Fearan from the court who was outside the house to give insight on what was happening and what they were looking to do.

Detective Gall was the lead investigator for the Milford police who were investigating this crime. Gall had not arrived on the scene before Cable, who was the first responding officer that discovered the victim. Chief Melo suggested to Detective Gall that they should have the state police come in with their major crime unit, which was agreeable to Gall because they had the whole team to do things.

Gall stated that he would stay on the scene to consult with the state police to provide anything that they may need and to answer any questions that they may have, concerning the investigation. Detective Gall remained on the scene with the state police the entire time that they were there.

Gall's initial crime scene incident report states that the date and time of the incident was Friday, May 19, 2006, at approximately 16:44. Milford Police responded to 3 Boothbay street to investigate a reported murder or suicide. Alexandra Ducsay was pronounced deceased at approximately 15:00. After clearing the house of other possible involved parties, the Milford Police secured the residence as a crime scene.

Members of the Connecticut State Police central district squad were requested to respond to the scene to assist with the scene processing. The State Police major crime scene unit did not arrive to the crime scene until 22:00 on Saturday May 20, 2006.

Gall arrived at the scene before the state police, and he stated that he stayed at 3 Boothbay Street initially until the state police showed up and photographed the outside of the house per our own investigative reasoning. Gall stated that he entered the house only minimally, to see what they had to deal with. Once the State Police had arrived at the scene, they took over the processing of the crime scene where the victim was found. Gall was able to investigate the crime scene from about 5pm or later until 10:10pm when the State Police finally arrived at the scene.

Detective Gall processed the crime scene for about 5 hours before the State Police arrived at the scene. He investigated the victim and evidence that was around the deceased in the basement. There were bloody shoe print impressions that left a pyramid type design, but this evidence was never documented in the report. This is apparent due to Detective Gall as lead investigator informing Detective Huggins of the Milford Police Department around 5:30pm or 5:45pm to check the suspects shoes for blood and a pyramid type design which was left at the crime scene.

In this investigation, there was never a forensic shoe print impressionist employed to reconstruct the print that was left to discover evidence that would have proved my innocence. I have to question the kind of investigating that was really done in this investigation. This was a homicide. Did they maliciously conceal evidence? Were the reports written in a way that kept the defense in the dark, stripping away the opportunity to put on a proper defense? One in which the jury may have returned a verdict of not guilty. Did the investigation become infected with tunnel vision only to focus on me, Matthew Pugh, as the prime suspect? All things considered; this investigation was a botched one to say the least.

In transcript from February 26, 2015, Prosecutor Kevin Lawlar states that the suspect cleaned up. He thought about it. He did not run out the door. No bloody footprints going out the door. This statement is proof positive that bloody footprints were found at the crime scene, but this bit of critical evidence was never introduced at the trial and the jury never got to hear it.

Was this a brazen attempt to undermine the rule of law and obtain a conviction based on lies? I would want to hear from Amy Bepko and Sunny Hostin of The View to answer this question, especially after finding out the additional fact of the case.

Innocent assistant, you watched me at the trial and if looks could kill, your stares alone could have sealed my fate. What you did not know was that when I caught eyes with you, I anxiously wanted to let you know that I would be back to tell the truth about the case and how blind your boss left you. This slap in the face undermines your intellect as a A.D.A which kept you on a string like a puppet. The orchestrated corruption made it easy to make it seem as if I was a monster, but when state agents conspire to obtain a wrongful conviction, who is really the monster(s)?

As far as Sunny Hostin, a former prosecutor herself, I could not believe that you did a show about my case that aired on the I.D channel (Investigative Discoveries). I personally did not see the show, but I was informed by a nurse who had seen the show and realized that she knew the person featured on the program. From what I have gathered, your show was also based on lies. You too did not and could not have known the complete truth concerning this case.

There should have been a thorough investigation done on your part to make sure that the state actors acted with integrity before misinformation is aired and is portrayed as the truth. Sunny Hostin, there are serious issues in my case that you reported on. What you did not report on was the withholding of evidence and the use of false testimony. The skills that you must employ as a prosecutor may have been on vacation at the time that you reported my case, but now that you have other platforms, such as Soul of a Nation and Truth about Murder, a real conversation about wrongful convictions and the prison industrial complex lingering effects on our communities can occur.

My question to you, Sunny Hostin, is whether it is right that a conviction is obtained by using lies and unfair tactics? I urge you to start the conversation about the flaws in the legal system and cause change to the known continuing injustices. Your celebrity status affords you a unique position to affect change.

As you read the next chapter of Hearsay or Fact, and the rest of the book Sunny, you will feel disrespected by how these officials used your status to bring light upon this case, when honestly, they love to put you on the same string as Amy Bepko, as well as to make you a puppet in their affairs of corruption.

CHAPTER 5

HEARSAY OR FACT

Police investigations, when done correctly, are commendable work. However, when the police start to suffer from tunnel vision, such as what was focused directly on me as the prime suspect, the investigators begin to forget to keep following that leads that they have which clearly led to an actual threat of violence. A close friend of Ms. Ducsay witnessed this threat while in her car—Jeremy Shoffner.

Direct Examination by Attorney Carty

Q: Okay. Did you at the time in 2006, have an acquaintance by the name of Alexandra Ducsay?

A: Yes, I did.

Q: Alright, how did you come to meet her?

I met her through a community choir from Weston.

Q. Alright, did you ever have an occasion to speak to her one on one?

A. Yes, I did.

Q. Alright, let me just back up a second. When did you meet her in 2006?

A. It was around February/March.

Q. February/March is when you met her?

A: Yes.

Q. Okay, can you tell us some of the things that you discussed with her?

A. It was more musical things involving songwriting pretty much.

Q: Alright, how did that topic come up?

A: I was sitting in her car, the Mitsubishi 300 GT, and I asked her, "You know, how did you get the car?" and she explained to me that she had gotten the money from someone and then we proceeded to have a conversation. I asked her if she had to pay the money back. She said that she could not pay the money back but that she had a couple of months to do so.

Q. How do you know that? How did you know that she had a couple of months to pay that?

A. Because that is what she said.

Q. Okay. Alright, did you continue discussing paying back that debt?

A. Yes, in so many words, she was asking me for help, and I said, at the time, I was working at Grace Baptist so I wouldn't—you know, I wasn't going to be able to help her, as I explained to her. I asked her if—you know—was she—you know—how are you going to pay for that? And I said, what if he comes after you—the guy that she got the money from and she—and her words were, "I'm not scared of that."

Q. Was she worried about it?

A. No.

Q. Okay, did she show you anything which would corroborate her—

A. She showed me a text message on her phone. A text message.

Q. Alright, what was the tenor of the text message?

A. It pertained to a threat, a life threat, that he was going to get her, and that was pretty much it. That was all I saw from the text message.

Q. Okay, what was your understanding of that text message?

A. That she was going to die.

Q: Now, you met her in February or March of 2006. About when in your acquaintance with her did this conversation take place?

A: I would say in May.

Q: Alright.

A: I'm sorry, I'm sorry, April.

Q: April?

A: Yeah, April.

Q: Approximately a month before she passed?

A: Yes.

Q: And you didn't offer any help? Did you continue to discuss that threat with her?

A: No, that was pretty much the conversation.

Q: Okay, had she ever mentioned an ex-boyfriend to you?

A: Yeah, she said she had one, the name of the ex was never mentioned to me.

Q: Okay, did she ever mention any threats from him?

A: No.

Q: So, at the time, really the only conversation you had was about that debt?

A: Correct.

Q: And how soon after the conversation where you learned that information about the debt did she die?

A: It was the day after my wedding anniversary, May 19th.

Q: Alright, how soon after the conversation about the debt was she found dead? What was the time period in between?

A: It was about a month.

Q: About a month?

A: Yeah, about a month—about a month.

Q: Okay, you do not know the person, but you did learn—did you learn the name of the individual?

A: Yes, I did.

Q: And what was that name?

A: She mentioned Donavan. That was the name given to me.

Q: Alright, thank you.

Q: Mr. Shoffner, you weren't personally acquainted with Donavan, were you?

A: No.

Q: Alright, was there—did you receive any other information about Donavan and the steps that he may have taken to come and collect the debt?

A: No, other than she got money from him to get that vehicle and that was who she owed money to. Other than that, no.

Q: I think I asked you whether or not during your discussion with Ms. Ducsay whether the subject of money being owed to someone came up.

A: yes.

Q: Do you recall that? And did it?

A: Yes.

Q: Okay, how did—how did that subject come about?

A: Because I asked her, you know, how she got the car.

Q: What car was that?

A: The 300 Mitsubishi 3000 GT.

Q: Alright, now why was this—was there something special about that car that would prompt a question like that?

A: Oh yeah. It was a nice car; expensive.

Q: Okay, so you asked her how she got the money for it?

A: Yes.

Q: And did she discuss the debt with you—the debt for the money to pay for that car?

A: Yes.

Q: Okay, and if you can tell us, was she able to pay that debt?

A: No.

Q: Alright, how did the discussion go with Ms. Ducsay?

A: Okay, she just—I said that was a nice car—you know, it was a nice car and asked, "You know, how did you get this?" She was like, "I got the money from this guy," and she named the guy.

Q: Right, then she named the guy?

A: Yeah.

Q. Alright, what was that name?

A: She mentioned Donavan.

Q: Do you remember the last name by any chance?

A: No.

Q: Alright, did she show you anything related to that?

A: As far as receipts or papers or something, or what do you mean?

Q: Anything that you saw referencing the debt?

A: No. No, as far as—no. That was—sorry. I am not sure what you mean.

Q: Okay, were there any messages back and forth between she and Donavan?

A: Not that—no, I didn't see any.

Q: Excuse me?

A: Not that was—no. The only message that was shown to me was a threat message of not—her giving the money back.

Q: Alright.

A: That was the only message.

Q: Okay. What kind of message was it? Was it a written message, a letter or—

A: A text message.

Q: A text message?

A: Yes.

Q: On her phone?

A: Yes.

Q: Alright, and you saw it with your own eyes?

A: Yes.

Q: Okay, and when did this conversation take place, approximately?

A: That month probably, maybe in the second—yeah, about a month—approximately a month before.

Q: Before she died?

A: Yeah.

Q: Okay, were you asked for help in terms of repayment of that?

A: Yes.

Q: Okay, did you provide any help?

A: No, I was not able to.

Q: And why was that?

A: Because I was not making enough money to help her with anything.

Q: What was her reaction to the threat that you observed?

A: She didn't seem bothered by it. She wasn't scared because that was her words to me. She was like, "I'm not scared of that."

Q: Alright, did you have any reaction to her reaction?

A: Yeah, I was shocked.

Q: You were shocked?

A: Yeah, that she wouldn't be—you know—fearful of her life you know? Being threatened like that, you know, especially with that amount of money.

Q: Did you know how much money it was?

A: It was in the area of $16 grand.

Q: And when you say $16 grand, is that—

A: Thousand. Sorry.

Q: Thank you. Did that—where were you when that discussion took place?

A: I was at—in Bridgeport at Dunkin Donuts.

Q: Dunkin Donuts?

A: Yeah, at Dunkin Donuts, not inside, just in the parking lot.

Q: At Dunkin Donuts, but in her car?

A: Right. Correct.

Q: Okay, did you continue your discussion with her?

A: On that subject, no.

Q: Yes.

A: No.

Q: Alright, during your conversation, did she mention her ex-boyfriend?

A: She mentioned she had one.

Q: Okay, she didn't mention that he was threatening or anything like that?

A: No.

Q: So, in the conversation, did you discuss anything other than a debt at the time?

A: No, we just went back to talking about music and songwriting.

Q: Okay, and how soon after that conversation did you learn that she died?

A: It was on that date.

Q: Excuse me?

A: It was actually the date that she died.

Q: Okay, how much time between the conversation that you had about the debt and the day of her death was there?

A: Approximately a month?

Q: Approximately a month?

A: Yeah.

Q: And you didn't personally know Donavan, do you?

A: No.

Q: Okay, you never met him?

A: No.

Q: Okay, you just know what you learned from the conversation with Ms. Ducsay?

A: Correct. Yes, correct.

Q: Alright. Thank you, I have no further questions.

Here we have proof by a defense witness who actually saw with his own two eyes the text messages that directly threatened Ms. Ducsay. Threatening that he would kill her if she didn't pay him back the $16,000.00 that he loaned her to purchase the Mitsubishi 3000 GT. The truth, it hurts, and in this matter, it is crystal clear. In the next chapter, The Truth Hurts, you will learn the truth too many events concerning this case that will prove that the police and states attorney only focused on me instead of following up on leads directly to the sender of the threats of death directed at Ms. Ducsay.

CHAPTER 6

SIGNS OF ENVY, ANGER, RESENTMENT & JEALOUSY

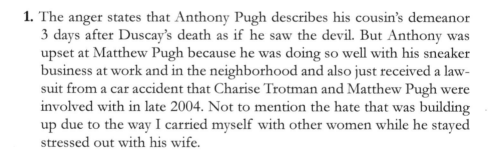

1. The anger states that Anthony Pugh describes his cousin's demeanor 3 days after Duscay's death as if he saw the devil. But Anthony was upset at Matthew Pugh because he was doing so well with his sneaker business at work and in the neighborhood and also just received a lawsuit from a car accident that Charise Trotman and Matthew Pugh were involved with in late 2004. Not to mention the hate that was building up due to the way I carried myself with other women while he stayed stressed out with his wife.

2. Purchasing my 300 ZX Twin Turbo should of raised a red flag when I came around the spot and Anthony Pugh wants to purchase the same car, so I still take him down to the Nissan dealer on Derby Ave and gives Ms. Susan who I knew a down payment to hold Herman Hans used Charcoal Gray 300 ZX twin turbo with a racing Tail Fin.

3. Even though my job Chromalley Ct. relocated to Windsor Ct. from Walling Ford and understand that I was an outstanding employee with the position I obtained in the clean room as a molder, they decided to thank me for my services with a $4 raise which I, in return, told them to split the $4 raise with my cousin Anthony Pugh who I just helped get hired at the job in Walling Ford Ct. due to Hamilten Connections temp service turning him down 3 times when tried to get a job at Chromalloy Ct.

4. A statement made by Anthony Pugh that he gathered by Chromalley Ct. due to his own self. When in fact I had to let my supervisor Pete and my boss know that the people that they were sending to me to train, couldn't keep up with the work, but I have a cousin who I train in my basement and is disciplined as myself and I recommend that you have him if you want to keep up with the demand. And they said to me, if he can work like you then call him right now and we'll have him. So I called Ant on his cellphone and let him know that I had good news and that I got him the job and to come to Walling Ford right now. But yet – his pride says he got the job on his own! It's funny how people's actions always exposes themselves!

5. When coming back from NYC with my order of sneakers and I stopped at Alexandra's house to give her some sneakers and an outfit outside of her porch in the front yard with her dog and when I left, a comment was made by Ant "you still deal with her?" Yea, why not, it wasn't her fault that we wasn't together, that was her mother doing. Zandra and myself were still good friends and dealing with each other.

6. While at work on 1st shift Anthony and myself would punch each other in the time clock if one of us got in to work before each other. Well on May 19th 2006 which was Friday, Anthony never came to work that day and he still was paid for it because I punched him in. But on Monday May 22nd 2006, I found out through him that he didn't come to work that morning because he told me himself but he lied to the police and said I looked like the Devil 3 days later.

7. I never really considered this until I began to think about the signs with Anthony. But I should of never invited you over so much when you didn't want to be around your wife Keisha and you would sit at the table with Charise and myself and eat dinner and work out in my basement because you were so stressed out by your wife.

8. When you lied to the investigations and to police about Alexandra meeting us at TownFair Tire in Orange Ct. because I wanted her to meet you and you said she really didn't want to be around, when on that same day that I dropped you off in West Haven, Zandra and myself headed to NYC together. After she parked her car at McDonalds on the I-95. But you never knew this because something always told me not to tell you everything and that's why you were so shocked when I popped up at her residence the day you took a trip with me to NYC.

It's sad that family has to envy my moves but I've been dealing with this my whole life so its nothing new. The scary part is that Anthony planned this because of his time he did at Rikers Island Prison.

You'll always be family to me but I want you to know this! You did 4 ½ years at Rikers for something you did and you should of listened to me and waited so I could deal with the connect personally. Also that 4 ½ years stressed you out that I see you was never built for the game. Yet the $ was good but when things go south you couldn't handle the consequences.

I've been incarcerated for 12 years now, stress free and I too am away from my children and family and in jail for something that I didn't do but yet I walk with my head up and do me because I know how to move in life when the tribulations and pressure seem to try and close off my greatness. But this is when you were suppose to hold it together because when you're blessed than there's no reason for you not to rise back up to the sky and let people know and see that the system never phased you.

Now I must show others that even though you tried to bury me alive, I still breath motivation, determination, will power, strength, spiritual guidance, compassion, forgiveness, loyalty, longevity, prosperity and faith that I will make it out of here by the Grace of God and taking this time to help my self out instead of whining or giving up. You thought you defeated me by your ill intentions but you've just made me that much stronger, wiser and successful.

You must not of known me that well because you would of known that I was a different breed! I forgive you CUZ! The question really is, would you have done what I'd done for you if the shoe was on the other foot? Your maggot ways could never stop my progression, for this is what I was created to do! It's my duty, obligation and responsibility to succeed.

Motivational Song - *"Sunshine"*
Latto Feat Lil Wayne/Childish Gambino

CHAPTER 7

THE TRUTH HURTS

If you followed this case from the states narrative and never came to know the violations that were committed to obtain this conviction, then it is possible to view me in a negative light. Does the exposure of the illegal acts committed by the state give you pause? Does it make you question the power the state has to prosecute a person, and on the other hand, abuse that power to obtain a wrongful conviction?

I have a motto that I live by which says: Does your word define you or do your actions expose you? If you follow this now, you will be able to understand how a true King or Queen knows how to move in a life of danger. The greatest power you could have in life would come neither from limitless resources nor consummate skill in strategy. It would come from a clear knowledge to distinguish friend or foe, real from fake.

Train yourself to read people by picking up the signals they unknowingly radiate which gives away their innermost thoughts and intentions. This knowledge helped me diagnose the actions employed by the state's attorney in his pursuit of a wrongful conviction. I took notes on all of the underhanded and unlawful actions so that one day, I would be able to expose the smoke and mirror show that takes place in courtrooms everyday all over this country.

One of these tactics was between the state's attorney Kevin Lawlar and Judge Denise Markle. A signal was used between the two to allow spontaneous excited utterance to be allowed over the objection to give the state a further advantage in obtaining a wrongful conviction. As we see, Jermaine Morton was on the phone with Ms. Ducsay around noon of May 19, 2006. They were discussing their plans for the night. Ducsay told Morton to, "Hold on, someone is at the door." Morton testified, "I could actually hear her in the background say, "What are you doing here? You were supposed to call first." She told Morton that she would have to call him right back and did call him back five to twenty-five minutes later.

During the second call or while Morton heard her statement the first time, he never heard her say, "my ex-boyfriend is at the door. No one was named and the conversation went on without anything being said that was out of the ordinary. The police changed Morton's 2006 statement from someone being at the door to her ex-boyfriend being at the door. This was denied on the stand, by Morton but the altered statement was given to the Jury as truth.

This was accomplished by the Judge giving a Whelan instruction. This rule allows prior statements to be entered into evidence even though certain evidence of this nature is not usually allowed to be heard by the jury. The State needed this confusion and deception to place me at the scene because not even the D.N.A could do it.

The argument that was made by my attorney on the allowance or denial of a spontaneous excited utterance seemed to be swaying the Judge to make her ruling in my favor, to keep this evidence out. The assistant State attorney's argument to allow this evidence was making no sense and was no where close to be on issue, when all of the sudden, I saw Kevin Lawlar, the states attorney, panic and give the Judge a signal that reminded her of whose side she was playing for.

This ruling allowed the case to proceed in a corrupted way that helped to strip away any sense of a fair trial. These are the games that are played everyday in this country.

I, Matthew Pugh, will give you the truth about my relationship with Ms. Ducsay. The State did not want the jury to know that we were on good terms even after being placed on seg for what was called a threatening letter, was received by her. The state objected to the truth, but I'm gonna give you the tea.

Direct Examination of Matthew Pugh by Attorney Carty

Q: Okay, and you were ultimately released from that sentence?

A: Yes, in August of 2004. August 6th.

Q: Okay, and had you received any extra time for having written that letter?

A: A couple of weeks. It didn't really do any damage.

Q: How did you feel about receiving extra time because of having written the letters?

A: I mean, I was upset at the time, but it didn't do any damage. I was—you know, Charise Trotman, she paroled me home, so I was okay…

Q: Okay. When you said Charise Trotman paroled you home, what do you mean?

A: Well, at that time, when I went to seg—I didn't know what was going on. My mind was baffled like, how am I going to get home? I really didn't want to go to no halfway house. But Charise's brother used to go to the church where my father was at and that's how she got in touch with me. I didn't go looking for Charise. Charise found me. So, it was not like I was looking for somebody else. It was just a blessing that she came through and I used to mess with her back in the day, twenty years ago, so that's how she paroled me home.

Q: Alright, so you knew her already, is that what you're saying?

A: Yeah, I knew her over twenty years.

Q: Okay, so you were paroled to Charise's home.

A: 98 North Street.

Q: Okay, when you got out, did you make any contact with Ms. Ducsay.

A: Yes, I did because it was still on mind like, what happened? We had a good relationship and everything. So, I called her, you know. I went to the Stop & Shop grocery store in Hamden, and I called Alexandra and she was surprised that I was out. She was so surprised that she came to Hamden to see me.

Q: Okay, and what happened then?

A: She hugged me, kissed me. She said that she was sorry.

Attorney Lawlar: Objection. Hearsay.

The truth hurts—and this is how Alexandra, and I handled our relationship when I came home. While we were together at the Stop & Shop in Hamden, she explained that her mother did not want her to be with me when she found out that I was home. That she was sorry for that. Alexandra wanted me to get into her car and suggested that we could get a room at a hotel.

I told her that I couldn't because I was now in a relationship with another woman, due to my situation at a level 3 facility, and that she paroled me home so that I would not have to a half way house. I told Alexandra to follow me in her car, so that I could show her where I was staying. We parked on 1st Street, and she jumped into my Acura, and we pulled onto North Street in Hamden and I showed her the house on North Street. She began to cry, and I told her that we could still be friends and that we would stay in touch with each other. That we would stay in contact regardless of my relationship with Charise.

Direct Examination By Attorney Paul Carty
Transcript February 18, 2015-Charise Trotman

Q: Okay, in response to a question by Mr. Lawlar, you had testified that you had confronted Matthew Pugh about calls from females.

A: Yes.

Q: On the phone that was actually in your name?

A: Yes.

Q: Alright, and you knew about that because it was on your bill, correct?

A: Correct.

Q: Okay, and were you aware of calls to and from Alexandra Ducsay?

A: Her and a couple of females.

Q: Did you speak to Alexandra Ducsay about her calling him on your phone, basically?

A: Once, but that was months before I ever had my daughter, I was pregnant at the time, and she had called once.

Q: That you were aware of?

A: That I was aware of.

Q: Alright, and you just answered the phone, or did you take the phone from Matt or what?

A: No. I had answered one time and asked her to stop calling him and she never did call back, to my knowledge.

Q: Okay, but she had been calling him more than that one time to your knowledge prior to that?

A: I don't recall. I mean, I don't recall.

Alexandra and I were still dealing with each other sexually and we would take trips to New York City. She would park her car at a McDonalds on I-95. I would drop her off back at her car after we did some personal shopping and some stuff for my sneaker business. Linda Ducsay never knew that her daughter was still dealing with me. Alexandra didn't mind our friendship and how we spent our time. She just wanted to be around me. She always blamed her mother for our breakup. Alexandra wanted me to parole to her mother's house, but her mother wouldn't allow it.

When Charise became pregnant, the relationship between Alexandra and me began to fade. I told Alexandra that I was going to marry Charise. I explained that she was a good woman and I wanted to make this relationship with Charise work. A key factor in that decision was the fact that Charise was having my baby. Alexandra did not take this news very well and at one point started to talk about suicide, and I told her that she would find someone that would make her happy and that it was not that serious that she would need to take her own life.

The Truth Hurts and the facts show that we were still friends and stayed in contact with each other. We even had codes with our car horns when we were outside of the others house so that we would not be found out by her mother or the mother of my child. When you want to see the person that you are involved with, there is nothing that is going to get in your way. Most people did not know or understand this truth. These are the ones who tried and continue to paint a different picture to what the relationship really was. Now, the truth has been told, so you can take it for what it is, for this chapter says—The Truth Hurts!

The trial was so corrupt, that even the family of the victim was blinded by the police and prosecutor's incompetence with this investigation, but I also have to ask myself, was the victim's family a part of the corruption as well? Since everyone was so focused on me as the one who committed this murder, the police had tunnel vision, the investigation turned up no fingerprints, no DNA, no blood in my Acura, and not a cut or any bruises on my body.

There was no forensic evidence to point at me as the one who committed this murder. It would have been telling if the police had found any evidence of my involvement when I willingly went to the Milford Police Department to be questioned from 5:45pm to 4:00am. While in the interrogation room, the Detectives investigating the case (Detective Youd, Gall and Sergeant Wydra) tried to get physical with me and create the illusion that they were willing to beat a confession out of me.

I told them to go ahead and that I could use the money. This statement threw them off their game plan and they backed off of me as they had me surrounded from all sides. This is an example of a bad investigation being handled from the place of emotion and not from the place of proper procedure.

Search Warrant

The police did not have the legal authority to come and question me at Papa John's or to ask me if I would come down to the station to answer some questions because the search warrant was not signed by the Judge until 7:40pm and the Detectives arrived at my second job at 5:30 to 5:40pm. This is proof that this search warrant was not officially signed, so the police had no right to and search my car, my sneakers, or question me on May 19, 2006.

On Friday May 19, 2006, a Judge signed a search warrant for the premises of 3 Boothbay street in Milford Connecticut 06460 at 7:40pm, giving the go ahead for the murder investigation to begin. This search warrant was also signed by Detective Roman who was Detective Arthur's boss at the Milford Police Department.

Detective Huggins and Detective Ron searched me for evidence of the presence of blood and a pyramid type shoe design that was left at the crime scene. All of this without a warrant which was not signed until 7:40pm on May 19, 2006. These actions are a clear constitutional violation, so I question the whole investigative process. Did the police disregard the rule of law to create a case? I would not be the first time. The Truth Hurts.

The next chapter is focused on envy, anger, resentment, and jealousy! Not only will this chapter explain Anthony Pugh's envy for me, but the reader will come to understand how he used deception to collect $50,000 from the state by using his false testimony to assist the state in obtaining a wrongful conviction against me.

MILFORD

Convicted killer's cousin up for $50K reward

Testified at trial over slaying of Alexandra Ducsay

By Phyllis Swebilius
pswebilius@nhregister.com
@pswebilius on Twitter

MILFORD » Superior Court Judge Denise Markle is due to rule today on a state request to give a reward of up to $50,000 to Anthony Pugh, who reluctantly testified at the murder trial of

Ducsay

his cousin, Matthew Pugh.

Matthew Pugh, 43, was sentenced to 60 years in prison May 11, nine years after he fatally beat and stabbed his former girlfriend, Alexandra Ducsay, 26, at her family's city home.

Anthony Pugh took the stand to describe his cous-

in's demeanor three days after Ducsay's death.

"He looked like he saw the devil," Anthony Pugh said at the February trial.

Anthony Pugh, then 41, testified he hadn't told everything he knew when police first interviewed him five days after Ducsay's death. "That was my cousin," he said in court.

"I didn't want to get involved in this. I didn't want to get involved in it now," he said from the witness stand.

Ansonia-Milford Judi-

cial District State's Attorney Kevin D. Lawlor filed a motion May 22 for Markle to release the reward.

Under state general statute, Chapter 960, Section 54-48, a person who gives information leading to the arrest and conviction of the guilty person may be eligible.

Matthew Pugh was identified as a "possible person of interest" the night of Ducsay's death, a retired police detective testified at

REWARD » PAGE 2

CHAPTER 8

ENVY. ANGER. RESENTMENT. JEALOUSY.

There was a time when I had to scramble in the streets. This was in the early 90's, when cocaine from New York City made it easy to stack paper from sales made around my hood. I purchased a black Twin Turbo 300 Nissan ZX in the early part of 1995. I still remember the days that I would pull up on the block where the setup spot and my cousins were located. I would do donuts in the middle of the street, and on most days the sun was working with me to help every penny of that $40,000 car shine just right.

To my surprise, my cousin Anthony Pugh suddenly got the urge to get one as well, but he was not making money like that to floss as hard as me. He must have remembered the time that I helped another cousin out when he was in a tight situation. He asked me to help him get the same car. I have always had made love for my cousin. He was my first cousin and we had always been close. Family has and will always be everything to me. I know he knew this, and he used this knowledge to get me to show him a bit too much love, because this made him look at my kindness as some type of weakness.

What I ended up doing for Anthony was taking him to the Nissan dealership and I let him pick out a charcoal gray 300 ZX with a racing tail fin. I took care of the down payment and told him that all he had to do was collect money from the workers and keep the spot supplied with cash. His task was simple, and I thought that when I had to take a trip out of state to handle something that I would not have to worry about anything.

I was wrong.

As soon as I reached my destination, Anthony called me to inform me that we were out of stock and the spot was booming with customers. I told him to hold tight and that I was on the way to collect and to hold the money so that I could hit New York City to see the connect. Anthony did not listen to me and took it upon himself to try and fix the situation. I guess because he got this 300 ZX, he thought that he could now do the things that I do.

For his rush to make a move, going to see the connect in New York City to purchase the weight himself, he was busted by the T&T drug task force while possessing all of the product on his person leaving the spot. He had to go to jail for four and a half years. Anthony could not be bonded out of jail because this arrest violated the supervision he was under. I know that he had ill-thoughts of getting back at me.

Anthony was blaming me for his actions, but if he really looked at the situation, he would have realized that the decision to go to the city was his and his alone. I felt that something was not the same when we saw each other years later. We came face to face at a homecoming party that my family had for me when I came home in 2004 after finishing a bid that I had caught.

I could see the envy and anger in his eyes that had developed while he spent time on Rikers Island. This made him very bitter. The love that I was getting from my other cousins did not help the jealousy that I saw bubbling up in him. I should have listened to my gut to put space between us, but family is everything to me, so I kept training Anthony and another cousin of mine in a basement.

At this time, Anthony and another cousin of mine were working at a fish market in West Haven. Through them, I got a job there too, working from 7:00pm to 7:00am packing tropical fish. That job was not for me, but we all have to do things that we do not want to do. I did that job for a very short time and lost interest even quicker. The single half hour break on the shift was a violation of labor laws and this helped to push me towards finding a better job. I walked off the job, but not before I told my cousins that if I find something better, I would plug them in.

I finally caught a break with a temp agency. They placed me at a job where I could not only make money but be trained to become a molder. I took this opportunity very seriously as I was working around engineers who depended on me to prep aircraft engine parts and to also inject rubber inside the parts so that they could move from the clean room where I was working and into the finishing staging area where the engineers would do their thing.

I worked harder than some people that were working at this place, so I was not surprised when I got promoted to molder over the person who trained me. I began training others that were slacking on the job. Thanks to this job, I was able to honestly purchase a four door Expedition for the mother of my child and a four-door green Acura TL for myself. Some people that I knew from the streets thought that I was back at it, but I was working hard and loving it.

My father had instilled into me a drive to achieve excellence, and this was what I was doing at this job. I knew that I could take care of my family doing this. The pay was good, my relationship was good, and the fact that my daughter was on the way was great, but it pays to pay attention to the dark clouds on the horizon because that is where the ones you show too much love to will wait to sabotage you.

Remember that I walked off the fish market job where my cousin Anthony and Eric remained? Well, Anthony had also left and was now selling vacuum cleaners door to door. I knew that he was not making the money that was needed to take care of his family. I also saw the envy continue to build in him as he would see how good my relationship was going and his was crumbling. He was continually having arguments with his wife. To avoid the madness, he would spend all of his free time at my house.

What he was seeing was me build my sneaker business while he could not figure things out. He possibly started to feel like less of a man as I continued to boss up. I knew that there was resentment for the arrest and time he did in New York, but I still got him a job where I worked, and

I spoke for him so that my bosses would give him a chance. I thought I was helping out of the hardship that he was in.

As he tried to keep up with me instead of working on himself and starting his own business, he came mad because I did not make him a partner in my sneaker venture. I would bring him to the city with me every re-up and give him a brand-new pair, but this was not good enough for him. I should have known from a comment that he made just how bad this resentment was getting. "I got my job on my own."

On the way back from New York City one day after a day of shopping, I stopped around the corner from Alexandra Ducsay's house at 3 Boothbay Street. I called her and told her to come out and get her present. She brought her dog and waited on the porch. I approached and gave her a pair of sneakers and a fly outfit. We still had a great thing between us, and this surprised Anthony. He asked me, "You still deal with Alexandra?"

I answered, "Why not, it's not her fault that I didn't get out of jail on time. It was her mothers doing and this time, her mother doesn't know that we are still dealing with each other."

After this, I really started to see the funny ways he was acting. The female traits that had picked up caused me to start blocking him out of my life. I soon was terminated from my job, and I was being investigated for the murder of Alexandra Ducsay. I moved back in with my father because the investigation was taking a toll on the mother of my child who had not had the baby yet and did not need the stress.

While I was living with my father, he reminded me of a lesson that he had been teaching me throughout my life. He said, "Son, I always told you that you never give up on life when obstacles and tribulations come into your path." I had to regroup and take another path. This path led me to a job at a pizza restaurant. The funny thing is that I started to make more money there than I had been making at the previous job.

I soon moved to Papa John's and after working there for a while, the police impounded my car sometime between May 24th and May 26th. This move could have put me out of work for a while, but like I have said, family is everything to me. My father and sister came together to make it possible for me to obtain her 2 door Acura, a standard that had better gas mileage. This came in handy because I had moved up to a better delivery service that had a better clientele and a better atmosphere to work in.

For a while, I did not know what happened to Anthony. When I found out about him again, he was deceptively fabricating a statement by the lure of reward to point the finger at me. The amount he sold me out for was $50,000. This was his chance to get back at me for his mess up in New York City and to come up money wise because he could never get his shit together to get it any other way. This is how weak rats live. They destroy everything that has been good to them and wait for the perfect time to strike.

I will never know what it feels like to lie to police, to pretend to be a concerned citizen who uses the states unrelenting power to enact revenge on a family member for things that I caused in my life. It hurt my heart to see the money being counted in Anthony's eyes as the lies came and continued to pile up. So, this is what it comes to? Helping these corrupt officials sentence me to a life sentence because of the resentment that built up in you because you could not do the things that I set out to do?

I will never come to understand why you would lie to bury me. Was what I did for you, give to you, and help you get not worth more than the blood money you received from selling your soul? I guess the bond of family means nothing and for you, I guess being a decent human being means nothing.

A perfect legal storm came down on me. Evidence was withheld from the jury, an incomplete investigation ensued, and a family member with a way to make easy money by selling lies to and for the state was ready to work.

In the next chapter, I will explain how I saw the loopholes and how I can use them to my advantage in further proceedings. Being attentive to the loopholes will give the attorney that champions my case the vision to see the corruption and a way to expose it to prove the malicious game that was played at my trial.

Motivational Song - *"Handle my Business"*
Migos/Culture III

"By the way, did the state <u>dismiss your threatening charge</u> in Wthersfield Ct., for cooperating with your deceptive lie in regards of 50,000 dollars? But yet, there were no favors in return?"

CHAPTER 9

THE LOOPHOLES

I started this chapter on my birthday which is June 19th. This day is now a federal holiday known as Juneteenth. I took this as a confirming sign from above telling me that I will be set free!

Most individuals that I have had conversations with about trials were too scared to deal with the real aspect that they may face one. Most ended up taking plea deals. I was steadfast about not letting the state control my thoughts through fear. I would not be their puppet on a string. This was the start of my focused journey which started with taking note of all the corruption that was affecting my situation.

On May 19, 2006, Detective Huggins and Detective Ron came to Papa John's on Whalley Avenue in New Haven, Connecticut. This was between 5:30pm and 5:45pm, when they told me that Alexandra Ducsay was deceased. The detectives also wanted to check my shoes for blood as well as the check the driver's side floor mat. I knew something was not right with what was happening.

To further their investigation, they asked me if I would come down to the station to answer some questions. I agreed without hesitation.

While at the Milford police station, I asked to call my attorney, Frank Antollino in Branford, Connecticut. This request was met with laughter, as I was told that I was not going anywhere. Hours passed before the detectives moved me to a tight interrogation room that had a long table and a chair that wobbled. They started to ask their questions. Who do I know that owns a red car, what do I do for work, where did I go on May 19, 2006?

They asked if I had seen Alexandra Ducsay or talked to her on May 19, 2006, and to this I answered no. They then asked me to remove my shirt. This was an attempt to see if I had any type of struggle evidence on my person. Not a scratch was found on me, and as I answered all the questions they had for me, the regret for coming to the station continued to steadily grow. A few questions had quickly turned into a hostile interrogation and all of this without my request for my attorney being respected.

This violation lasted from 6:00pm to 4:15am. Due to this investigation, the mother of my child was harassed which put a strain on how much I could see my daughter. She, like most people, did not know that you can tell the police to stop the harassment and if they don't, you can file a charge against them.

The information that I gave was not taken. I guess that she too thought that I was guilty, but how could she know how corrupt the detectives were? How could she know of the evidence that was being hidden from the crime scene? Or of the falsely taken statements from the one who would become the states star witness? All in order to obtain a wrongful conviction.

They treated her like she had committed a crime, and the fear that I saw in her eyes fueled me to fight this case to the very end. All things now considered, there is no way that should have cooperated at all.

Fast forward to 2015, the place is the courtroom where my trial is taking place. From the start, there were issues with the case. Jury misconduct happened when a juror knew the victim's cousin, "Brenda," and admitted that she worked with her. Removal of this juror would have been the correct thing to do but this trial was not about a fair judicial process being afforded to me. This trial was about closing a cold case with the help of a snitch who was awarded money for the testimony that was provided.

It was very difficult to sit still and continue to be respectful as my defense attorney's representation. I watched in disbelief as the state was being handed an easy win. I have always asked myself if the other eleven jurors knew that there was a biased juror among them, that she knew the victim's cousin, and that this connection may have colored the waters of this jury deciding the case? I wonder that the jury was hearing from this juror during the deliberations, and I also wonder how the presiding judge allowed this to happen in her court.

I had to place a great amount of focused attention on the ways that the state was breaking the law such as how the judge rushed the case so that the holiday season would not be infringed upon, as well as the loopholes that I would need to beat the case in further proceedings. I saw firsthand how the state will and does lie, cheat, and make up and hide evidence to obtain a conviction. All of this with consequences because of the protection that shields them from suit and charge no matter what they do.

I knew that I had to fight for me as no one else was. You might say that the lawyer was fighting also. Well, if he was, how was he in a fair fight when he did not even know of the things that were kept away from him? I wonder how an attorney does not know that a charge that the state was bringing against me was way past the statue of limitations? This is elementary.

Further, how could a seasoned trial attorney not notice that a detective was committing perjury about watching a Hess gas station surveillance video? I had to begin taking notes on body language. Due to where I come from, I could see that the detective that was giving testimony displayed an unsteadiness in his character. What I saw in him bothered me so much that I was able to see the orchestration between him and the states attorney. I kicked my attorney under the table and told him that this detective was lying about what was seen on the surveillance video. He responded by asking, "What do you mean?" This further strengthened my truth that I could not depend on an attorney that could not prove to a jury that this detective was committing perjury on the commands of the state's attorney when the proof was available to be discovered.

I had to remain composed in this situation and use this time to sketch a strategy that would be my defense in the future. I lost the trial and had to deal with that reality, but I knew deep down that I would eventually win. I honestly believe that nobody or anything can block my victory.

In the next chapter, never believe in defeat. I will give you my vision on how I see this moment happening and why keeping peace of mind helped me to control my emotions while dealing with disappointing events.

CHAPTER 10

NEVER BELIEVE IN DEFEAT

*"He leads counselors away plundered,
And makes fools of the judges." (Job 12:17)*

I t is May 11, 2015, and the atmosphere in the courtroom feels dead and cold. In my mind, I am processing the thoughts that I have had of the way that I have been set up from the start of this investigation. My thoughts also jump from the judge, states attorney, my attorney, and this bias juror that was not removed from the panel.

I then sit back into the chair and begin to read The Power of Positive Thinking by Norman Vincent Peale. This action was one of my ways to remain calm, collected, and confident about returning to this courtroom once the world has learned about this wrongful conviction. Yes, I wanted to be found not guilty on all counts. As the judge was reading off each count from the jury form that was handed to her by a court official, I was saying to myself that the world needs to know about the corruption that infected this courtroom.

"Matthew Pugh, you are sentenced to 60 years to life!" Seemingly unmoved, an out of body feeling came over me and I saw myself let out a huge yawn and stretch my arms to the sky. I then heard myself say that this is boring, just wait until I am back to prove and uncover the corruption that helped secure this wrongful conviction. This exposure will show that government officials did in fact use their positions of power to abuse the law and obtain yet another wrongful conviction.

With knowledge of investigations that are not done right, corruption that infects the legal system and the protection that is afforded to those who obtain wrongful convictions, then an understanding of how persons in power can control a case by the evidence that is presented being in their favor and the evidence that would help a defendant misplaced, lost, or destroyed. Some people still believe that the legal system has something to do with justice. My intention is to reveal the corruption that infects so many courtrooms all around this country. I will prove to you with the facts from this case, that corrupt officials are real and crooked state attorneys really do exist.

Wrongful convictions happen more often than many may think. The facts will have those who read this book asking why this was done to him. Why didn't he get a fair trial when the state had all the evidence to grant a fair trial as secured the United States Constitution? I encourage you to pay close attention to the case so that you will understand that wrongful convictions happen often and there are many people spending decades in prison away from loved ones, chances, and life all together. Many people believe this to be true. I believe that they have not yet been introduced to these tragedies. I continue to work to fight the good fight.

The work is to open the minds of those who are closed off. Some might say that it is impossible to win my case, but many things that were once impossible are now possible. My faith has kept me through this journey. It has been my attitude that has kept my head above water. I had positive energy during my trial and sentencing, and this is how I will get through the things that are next to come.

I have not been broken from being sentenced to 60 years, so what is there that I could not endure? I have been ready for this before this came into my path. God leads me and I find comfort in the Word. I have built a spiritual connection with Him which sustains me through this hostile place and all the tribulations that I face daily. I move with faith. God sees and knows what I am capable of handling. In life, I had to see things before they took place, which allowed my defense to be ready for what did come. I plotted my strategy mentally at trial as my attorney and his attorney friend were acting like little kids discussing the firm that they were going to open in Hamden Connecticut after they beat my case.

It was due to this selfish planning that he could not focus on trying to save my life. How could I trust an attorney that did not have my best interest on his mind? I even filed a complaint with the grievance board claiming that Paul Carty was in fact ineffective as trial counsel when he represented me at my trial. I made this claim based on the fact that he did not remove or excuse the 12 Juror from the panel.

I know exactly what happened at trial. I know the words that were said between he and I. I filed the complain in good faith, the following is the actual letter that Paul Carty sent to answer the grievance, misinforming the board of what happened in the courtroom.

Law Office of Paul V. Carty

233 Orange Street
New Haven, Connecticut

Mail to: P.O. Box 3192
New Haven, Connecticut 06515-0292

phone: 203-387-5400
fax: 203-387-5402

April 9, 2015

Michael A. Georgetti, Esq.
67 Russ Street
Hartford, CT

Re: Pugh v. Carty/#15-0186

Dear Attorney Georgetti:

I am writing in response to the grievance complaint filed by Matthew Pugh. I was assigned to represent him as a Special Public Defender in September, 2012 for charges arising out of a "cold case" murder of one of Mr. Pugh's former girlfriends in Milford, Connecticut. It goes without saying that any murder case is complicated, and must be taken with the utmost of care, as the consequences of a misstep are potentially devastating. What we have here is a case which had gone virtually nowhere for six and one half years before the state obtained a warrant for Mr. Pugh's arrest. The evidence file was extensive, and had been doled out piecemeal. Nonetheless, whatever time was needed to review the file was given it by me. I also engaged the services of an investigator, Kenneth Novi, who had been working on a robbery/assault case that Pugh has pending in New Haven, where he is represented by Attorney Thomas Farver. I had figured that it was better to work with someone who already had a relationship with the defendant, rather than to reinvent the wheel.

In any event, I appraised Mr. Pugh of the state of the file and the investigation, at every step of the proceedings. I also tried, I believe, two murder cases while this case was pending, in addition to several trials of lesser severity. This case was supposed to have been called in during the spring of 2014. However, it should be noted that this matter was pending in Milford, and that there is but one criminal trial judge sitting there. She had a number of other trials while this case was pending. I was comfortable enough with the state of the case and our investigation, such that a motion for speedy trial could have been filed last summer, but, as I explained to Mr. Pugh, it is usually better to let a case of this age sit on the trial list, since witnesses may become unavailable, forgetful, or their versions may change sufficiently to provide fodder for my cross examination.

The case was called in for jury selection in early-mid January, 2015. Prior to that time, I re-read the entire file, and continued doing so throughout jury selection and, as to relevant portions, during evidence. I also formulated several theories of defense, some of which fell apart based upon the time lines established at trial. However, other theories of defense were rock solid, even before the defense had an opportunity to present evidence. During jury selection, as to each venire person, I consulted with Pugh prior to accepting or rejecting a potential juror. He speaks of juror #12 as one who I failed to discharge. She was not discharged because, after consultation with him, it was decided that she would "play it straight" and in doing so, we would be assured that he would get the benefit of the doubt. He says that I ignored him and his requests. I have to say this is a flat out lie. With any potential juror with whom he felt uncomfortable,

A Conviction Based Upon Lies

he would give me the "sign", and he/she would be summarily excused. This is how I coordinated with him, and is the way that I would always coordinate with my clients when on trial.

With regard to being prepared, while I pride myself in being prepared for any case I am called upon to try, preparation in this case was extreme. Days, nights weekends, and what have you went into the preparation of this case for and during trial. I recognized that this was a wholly circumstantial case, and that the circumstances, taken together, could conceivably form a box around Mr. Pugh. My job was to open the box, and/or keep it from being closed in the first place. As to each of the state's pieces of evidence, I had an answer. As to each circumstance, I had an alternate theory based upon the evidence, right down to the fact that the police failed to process certain DNA-laden evidence found on the body, and as to the DNA evidence actually presented, a concession from the state's expert that the evidence was not conclusive, and testimony from my expert that the DNA evidence as it was could not place Pugh in the victim's house beyond a reasonable degree of scientific certainty. Additionally, there was a purported "eyewitness", whose credibility I was able to totally eviscerate. The state had evidence from a "cell tower expert" purporting to place Pugh's phone in a geographical area close to the victim's home. However, he had to concede that Pugh could be anywhere within the coverage area of a particular tower, and he could not place him at the victim's home. I was even able to get testimony in regarding a potential third party perpetrator, which was buttressed by the state's failure to have the evidence from the body tested.

In essence, the case was in its best position for either a mistrial or an acquittal when I was done. Be that as it may, although Mr. Pugh had repeatedly said he was not going to testify, the Monday prior to the close of evidence he contacted me and said he "had to" testify. He "had to tell his story". I advised him strongly against it. In fact, for two days I tried to talk him out of it. I did not give the state a heads up about it, because that would give the prosecutor more time to prepare. Up until the point that he took the stand, I was trying to get him to remain silent. But he would not. He handed me a list of more than 50 questions to ask him. I pared the list down significantly, and tried to limit areas of inquiry, such that I could limit cross examination to the greatest extent possible. When I was done, I had the distinct feeling of watching a train wreck, and the wreck of everything that I'd spend the previous two months developing. To say that his cross examination was ugly is to be extremely understated. To make it worse, it was completely unnecessary, at least from a defense standpoint. It was a gift to the prosecution.

The jury deliberated about 2½ days prior to reaching a verdict. They requested playback of much of the trial testimony. As to each of the witnesses, the testimony bore out exactly what I said it did in my closing argument. Things were looking great for Mr. Pugh. The last thing they requested was the playback of Pugh's testimony. It is clear that his testimony was the reason they came back with a guilty verdict. After retiring to the deliberation room once they heard Pugh's testimony, a verdict was reached in less than ten minutes. I had the jurors individually polled. Of note is the fact that, while this was going on, Pugh stood next to me with a big, arm stretching yawn. It most definitely looked out of place and inappropriate. One thing that the prosecutor said afterwards is that he would not think of going on to Pugh's turf and running the show. What makes Pugh think he could run the show on his turf? This was a major miscalculation on Pugh's part, and it cost him likely the rest of his life.

It bears saying that, for someone who was "not prepared", all observers in the courtroom, and of the news media, said that I'd done a masterful job, even though Pugh was convicted. I can't tell you how many of my colleagues and members of the public have come up to me and commended me for a job well

Pugh v. Carty
April 9, 2015
page three

done. I was even approached yesterday by a man whom I don't know, but who had watched some of the trial in Milford at the courthouse, and followed it in the papers. He felt compelled to shake my hand to commend the job the job that I'd done. What's more, Mr. Pugh wrote me twice after the trial to thank me for the thorough, professional job that I'd done. (Copies are attached).

Without getting into everything that Pugh testified to, he stated that he'd left work early on the day in question so he could spend time with one of his girlfriends – who was not available at that time. He decided to "surprise" another girlfriend for lunch, but she could not get out of work. Thus he created a reasonable inference that, if he tried to surprise girlfriend 1 with a visit, and tried to surprise girlfriend 2 with a visit for lunch, who's to say he did not try to surprise girlfriend 3 (the victim) with an unannounced visit. Further, while the cell tower evidence was flawed, in that Pugh's phone could be anywhere within a 1.5 – 2 mile radius of any cell tower that it hits, he placed himself within a half mile or less of the victim's home during the relevant time period. I spoke to the prosecutor this morning, and he related that two prosecutors from his office had gone out for coffee after the verdict, and ran into the foreperson of the jury. What she said was that many, if not most, of the jurors were not sure that Pugh had even been in Milford – until he testified. That tells me that he may well have been acquitted, but for his having taken the stand. What he did was to snatch defeat out of the jaws of victory, for which he has no one to blame but himself.

In light of the foregoing, it is quite evident that I did my job to the absolute best of my ability. If it were permissible to bind and gag him to keep him off the stand, I might have done so. Since it is not permissible, everything that could have been done on Pugh's behalf was done by me, and his grievance complaint should be dismissed, inasmuch as it is totally without merit.

Very truly yours,

Paul V. Carty

As you can see, the letter does not add up to what happened at the trial. Juror #12 reported to the Court that she knew and worked with the victim's cousin in Southbury, Connecticut. She was the last juror picked, which caused pushback against the removal of this juror because the Court had already given the panel a time in which the trial would take, as to not interfere with the holidays. Due to this, Paul Carty tried to convince me that she would be great for the defense.

I was reluctant and kept telling him that I did not like the way in which she kept looking at me, and that I did not feel comfortable with her on the jury. He thought he was managing the situation by choosing Juror #12, but I saw and felt that this was a major mistake. Other mistakes that he made were not presenting relevant defense evidence, such as the gas attendant and a footprint expert. An attorney is to have effective communication with the client that they are representing. This communication was lost with Carty and I. He disregarded the information that I was giving to him and ran with some other theories that he believed might win the case.

If trust was established with this attorney, I may have been more open to his antics, but when an attorney fails to discredit a detective that is giving false and misleading testimony that was clearly orchestrated by the state and also fails to be aware of a charge that the state is trying to place on me that was way past the statue of limitation, how can one have trust and belief while watching said attorney perform below the standard of effectiveness? I had to kick this attorney under the table to wake him up to the goings on in the courtroom. What was I to think about the level of concern that this attorney had for me and my situation?

I had to get on the stand and tell my story, because this attorney did not do it for me. The full story could not be told because the level of investigation and preparation were subpar at best. How could you have not known about the bloody footprints that were withheld from the reports. Find the answer to this may have won the case for me. I was not pleased with your representation, and your actions show the level of your performance. Not your level of representation, but the level of your performance, because what was done as your "job" was nothing more than that.

There is a problem with actual performance and representation and what is being allowed to pass in the courtrooms as this. The public tends to be blind to this fact, even the ones that sit on juries. The system works all good and well until they or someone that they love is forever changed by the system. My situation is not special. Justice is being perverted everywhere and every day. I am doing my part in informing the public by writing this book about the real workings of the injustice system!

Ineffective assistance in the courtrooms is becoming the norm. By this, justice cannot be called justice. This perverted acceptance of subpar representation is the crumbling of what is guaranteed under the Constitution and to our fellow man. I may be the only one that sees it this way, but then again, I am a different breed!

Trust with counsel is fundamental, competency in an attorney is a requirement. The attorney that represented me at trial might say that if I did not take the stand then I would have won the case. I disagree because he had many other chances to win the case, starting with the investigation. Since I felt that he was not doing everything that he could to win my case, I felt that I had to get on the stand to tell my truth. It was his job to get the jury to hear about the evidence that was withheld from the defense. I had all the legal antics that were happening, if I could not do this than I would have asked, "if I say to corruption, you are my father, and to the worm, you are my mother, and my sister. Where then is my hope? As for hope, who can see it?" (Job 17:14-15).

When God is for me, who can be against me? Part of my testimony is my calm behavior when being sentenced to 60 years to life because I had peace in the storm and still hold a clear vision. I can speak of about my journey to all that have lost hope in the system. Stark reality awakens the soul to fight for what is next. The next chapter will shock the mind as these are truths that will never be forgotten. This book will leave an impression In Your Mind.

CHAPTER 11

IN YOUR MIND

While I was on the stand, I gave brutally honest truths about the challenges of surviving and what I had to endure on the streets due to social constraints. I often ask myself what the Jury wanted to hear from me? Was I to get on the stand and commit perjury or fabricate a life that was not true to the one that I lived?

The sentencing judge on May 11, 2015, stated, "after reviewing all of this on paper and looking at it and finding it quite disturbing and seeing a substantial criminal record, however, the most disturbing evidence of your criminal activity, actually, Mr. Pugh, came from your mouth when you chose to take the stand and you testified under oath. Without being questioned by either the state or your own attorney, you voluntarily and freely offered testimony of your engagement over the years involved with criminal activity and the sales of narcotics, both in the state of Connecticut and in the state of New York."

She continued, "You gave this court a clear impression that you were proud and confident in that role and you appeared either—either—I don't know how to interpret it, but I have watched many people testify under oath, and it appeared to me that you were either outright defiant, or if I gave you the total benefit of the doubt, oblivious to the fact that any of your conduct was wrong, illegal, and that your actions just seemed to be a part of your life and anti any authority and inability to even comprehend the laws that we have in our society and a total disregard to any rules that protect our society."

I asked very politely anyone who judged me about the reality that I had to survive in or about my decision to get on the stand to tell my truth. Other than what I did to survive and in defense of my life? Did my testimony negate the misleading and false narrative that was used to convict me? My testimony did not please the judge, so the shady issues attached to the investigation which led to this wrongful conviction make this violation okay? I have presented issues against the police and state and have explained how my due process was violated.

Was there a fair trial here? I still ask why didn't the judge simply remove the questionable juror? Could this juror sit and still be fair after responding yes to working with the victim's cousin? I wanted the juror to be removed but my trial attorney convinced me that this juror would be good for my defense. This was not a strategic move; it is a clear example of an action that falls below the level of competence that a defense attorney is required to provide their client. My Constitution rights were violated.

CHAPTER 12

ADDICTED TO THE CHALLENGES

Fear is the primary motivating factor of sheep and slaves that never tried to regain their freedom. There are many prisoners that are asleep. The awakening of the truth has not happened within them and hope has been lost. Hopelessness encourages an ignorant mind which causes a state of doubt and confusion. Absent thinking allows comfort to be locked in a cage when thoughts of fighting for freedom should encompass all thoughts.

I knew on July 14, 2010, when I was incarcerated by the New Haven Police department that they were helping the Milford Police to build a case against me. This tactic vexed me so much that I decided not to use the phone to call my loved ones. What I did was write to them so that they could have my words and character on paper. These words were of love and encouragement so that they, in their freedom, be free because there are so many that have actual freedom that are not free.

I gave them the gift of words that were intended to promote positive thinking and the truth about keeping faith in God, knowing that we will never be given more than we can handle. The system thought that by breaking me down physically, they would break me mentally. But I found peace. How, you might ask, could peace be found in a prison? My answer is having a spiritual connection with God and paying attention to the signs that he allows me to see. This connection took much effort on my part and a belief that God has a plan for me. This allows me to be on this journey always progressing.

I have been ticket free for 11 years and I haven't touched the recorded phones for just as long. I am content with just doing me and writing to my loved ones. My main objective is to regain my freedom and bring the "how I did it" to others that are seeking the same. I also challenge myself with daily workouts which has become my saving grace, with a rush that comes with it. I want to give the world these challenging workouts that have helped me. A great source of power that keeps me energized in this hostile and negative atmosphere; I believe that these workouts can do the same for you.

Do not let stress get the best of you. Working out can combat the levels that stress can climb to. Do what you can with these workouts until you can keep up and I am confident that the rush will keep your mind calm, and your body will feel completely different. These workouts last only for 15 minutes, so let us try to stay within this time limit. Do not feel discouraged. The workouts are challenging and different and are designed to wake the mind and body by disrupting the normal boring programmed workout. The fighter within you will awaken, lets get to the rush!

Here are two weeks' worth of sets that will challenge you mentally and physically. Pick a routine that works for you or jump right in and challenge yourself with them all.

15 Minute Motivation—Week 1

Day 1
  50 Straight flat pushups.
  50 Straight mountain climbers
  50 Squats
  100 Jumping Jacks
  50 Push-ups off step or chair-straight
  50 Mountain climbers-straight
  100 Calf raises-straight

20 Close grip pullups
25 Dips straight
50 Mountain climbers-straight
10 Wide pushups
25 Dips straight
50 Pushups straight

Day 2
100 Pushups straight
100 Squats straight
4 Sets-25 Diamond pushups
25 Mountain climbers super set
2 Sets pullups hanging leg raises 10 reps feet touch bar
2 Sets 1 arm pullups-Super set grab wrist tight-5 reps each arm.

Day 3
50 Dips straight
50 Lunges each side straight
50 Hanging knee high straight
50 Mountain climbers straight
2 Sets-50 pushups off stool or chair straight.

Day 4
50 Flat pushups-50 calves
50 Flat pushups-50 calves
50 Arms 50 Arms
100 Tick Tocks
50 Arms each side
50 Pushups off chair or stool

"There's great power when materializing what you can achieve."

"Visualize your calmness and awareness."

For motivational support, I would prefer you to be self-motivated, but if you lack this, I suggest that you use your minds eye to imagine the workout being completed by your drive and efforts. Incorporate your best motivating music to gain the effectiveness that your body is capable of when handling an intense program. I am convinced that you will surprise yourself with the progress after completing the goals.

Day 4 Continued
   50 Jumping Jax
   50 Arms
   50 Squats
   15 Straight leg raises/15 calves

50 Pushups off stool-50 pushups flat

Day 5
50 Burpees double pushups straight
2 Set mountain climbers (50) straight
100 Squats straight
20 Close grip under hand pullups straight

Day 6
4 Sets 10 reps close grip pullups
4 Set Super Set 25 mountain climbers
10 Reps wide pushups/10 reps' diamond
pushups back & forth until you reach 100 reps.
10 Lunges on each side
20 Squats10 Jumping Jax squats-stay on the balls
of your feet—never let your heels touch the floor
10 Boxing steps squats Super Set bouncing feet
front to back.
Do 100 reps all together with both/do regime
twice, finish workout with 20 reps close grip pullups
straight/50 reps mountain climbers

Day 7
Stomach 9 sets off pull up bar
15 Reps straight leg raises
15 Reps knee ups
Every other set switch up until
you reach 9 sets the 10th is 50 reps of
knee ups straight.

Remember that these workouts are a challenge. If you can not complete them in 15 minutes, keep practicing until you master the task. If there is a routine that you gravitate to, use the regime to help you build your strength so that you can experience the rush while rising to the challenge.

These workouts will increase your metabolism drastically so make sure that you eat after you cool down. There is no diet plan with these workouts. They are designed so that you can eat whatever you want. I predict that if you can master these workouts, then you will not have a problem with your weight, cardio, strength, or appearance.

One might say that these workouts are too much, and the average person cannot handle this regime. I anticipated this so I took an average person that was not working out and put him to task. As he worked out, I began to evaluate his progress. My boy John John is now completing these workouts with ease. His results are noticeable to all. It took determination and focus to get to the level of master.

He did it and so can you. Do not ever speak the word CAN'T! This is a defeating mind set that will exclude you from your progress that you can be making. Take each play day by day, see yourself progressing with each rep and each stage. Leaders finish with success. Are you a leader?

My name is BREED in here. This is because I am different in the way that I move. I have structured my mind and thought process to not allow average issues break my focus or trigger the emotions in me. I do not let this system that is designed to retard the mind and decay the senses , to erode me. I visualize myself in my own world doing what I want, and I block out any petty issue that comes to disturb my world.

Every cell has its own atmosphere that is dependent on the relationship that you have with the person living in the same space. I am in the cell with my boy John John and the mood is laid back and relaxing. I am sure that some people are asking, "How could you relax and get comfortable while doing so much time?" My answer to that is if I am not able to relax then I will fall victim to everything that the system is designed for.

Week 2

<u>Day 1</u>
   50 Mountain climbers straight
   2 Sets 10 Close grip pullups/10 wide pullups
   50 Pushups off stook straight
   50 Calve raises straight
   50 Squats/10 wide pushups straight
   25 Dips straight
   20 Pushups flat straight
   50 Pushups flat straight (15 to 30 seconds breaks)
   30 Pushups flat straight
   50 Mountain Climbers straight

<u>Day 2</u>
   3 Sets 30 reps on each arm
   2 Sets of 50 Mountain climbers
   2 Sets 25 regular burpees
   100 Jumping Jax
   20 Close grip underhand pullups
   100 Pushups flat straight
   100 Calve raises straight

<u>Day 3</u>
   10 Down knee-high cross to elbows
   55 Reps total standing up
   100 Pushups flat straight
   50 Mountain climbers straight
   50 Dips straight
   4 Sets Diamond pushups 25 Reps each
   20 Reps straight close grip
   underhand pullups
   50 Mountain climbers

<u>Day 4</u>
   5 Sets Spiderman pushups 10 Reps
   on each side. Be sure that your knees
   touch your elbows when going into

your pushup stance
100 Calves
2 Sets of 50 on each arm

Day 5

5 Sets of 50 flat pushups Super Set with 5
sets of calves (50 Reps)
6 Sets of Pushups off stool Super Set with
6 sets of mountain climbers 10 reps each
100 Reps flat pushups straight. If you can not finish, in
15 seconds continue until you reach 100.
2 Sets of reps straight of close underhand grip
pullups
100 Calves straight

Day 6

(Put support under your back for 100 leg raises/prefer on bed or Mat)
100 Leg raises straight-laying on your back
100 Tick Tocks side to side straight
20 Burpees with double pushups straight
50 Squats straight
15 Lunges on each side straight

Day 7

Rest. Best results are achieved by doing the proper formation.
Make sure each rep is completed, not half done. If you
want to experience with your body an amazing experience,
Do not Cheat.
Major Challenge
5 Sets 5 reps of pullups over the bar
Superman pullups.
5 Sets 15 Rep Super Set hanging knee-ups
3 Set 10 Reps with stomach wheel standing up.
If you are a beginner, do 3 sets of 30 reps
with wheel on knees.
EXTREME CHALLENGE
100 Pushups straight
100 Jumping Jax

Do this five times. Both sets count as one set. You should have completed 500 pushups and jumping jax. Try to finish this in less than a ½ hour. It is the duty of the system to give me a challenging time on this journey. It is my duty to not let that happen.

I normally prepare delicious meals for John John and myself to escape from this world for a while. These meals allow us to have the feeling that we are enjoying a meal in a fancy restaurant. Jerk pork, yellow rice with beans, BBQ imitation rib tips with a fish wrap laced with provolone cheese, onions, garlic, and a sweet sauce. Something different might be my favorite. Stewed chicken loaded with jerk pork with provolone cheese in the wrap with pepperoni mixed in the yellow rice and beans.

There is also a unique and extraordinary meal I chef up which is my delicious chicken parmesan with black beans and corn in the Spanish rice. Seasoned red potatoes are smothered on top of the tomato sauce with provolone cheese. These meals are intended to give any pessimistic individual behind these walls a sense of hope and of freedom in their mind set after a taste of this seasoned blessing. These meals help me sleep well, so that I can be in touch with my dreams and visions which keep my soul filled with joy and relaxation.

My adversary's have only made me stronger, as I have gained wisdom that has allowed my strategy for freedom to come together. The next chapter is titled Continue to be me-My way. I wrote this book to give a glimpse of what my journey through this whole legal nightmare has been like and to show that even though I am surrounded by hostility, negativity, lost hope, bitterness as well as great amounts of tension that is always building up no matter how positive my energy may be flowing from me.

Motivational Song -"*I Told You/Another One*"
Tory Lanez

CHAPTER 13

CONTINUE TO BE ME—MY WAY

In this world, there are leaders and followers. Which one are you? Regardless, if you are doing time or in the real world, there is a choice to be made about these positions. I learned from a leader how to uncover and use the flaws that were present in my trial for murder. Is it odd that I had to listen and learn from someone in a situation like mine? I say yes because if I had listened to the bad information that I was given from a practicing trial attorney, I would not have been able to make any progress with the errors and corruption that happened in the courtroom as if it was legal.

I believe that the most powerful force in nature is the spiritual one contained in the Bible. I place emphasis upon this belief because with this understanding, one can find the strength to make something out of themselves. I also believe that with faith, belief, and positive thinking one is able to believe that people are good and that you are worthy and meant for great things because, *"If though canst believe, all things are possible to him that believeth,"* (Mark 9:23). *"If ye have faith...nothing shall be impossible to you,"* (Matthew 9:29). Believe.

I believe that faith does move mountains. I have gained much from these verses and have come to understand that God has all the answers including the answer to the most difficult questions and the simplest questions. I was doubted in my belief that one day I will be free again as I was sentenced to a great amount of time.

The doubt is understandable, but as I sat in that courtroom chair reading The Power of Positive Thinking, something deep down in my soul made me relax and I just knew that God was preparing to make a miracle happen with amazing results. It was my faith that gave me the strength to believe that the best was still to come, and the worst was put out of my mind. Eventually, I know that I will have the victory. The first trial was just a stumbling block, that most saw as a defeat. In that sentencing moment, I had to lean on all the faith that I had. This was a difficult time, and I needed my spiritual essence to lead my physical self to victory.

I was comforted by God at my sentencing and in this horrible time, I did smile a little inside knowing that my connection with God was growing stronger. I said to myself, they are going to be shocked when I return to this courtroom when my innocence is finally proven, and the light is shown on this wrongful conviction.

Through it all, I continue to be me and handle things my way! It is a wonderful feeling to know that everything is handled with certainty in my situation. My victory will be a testament of what having faith in God can do. This is not a cavalier statement rather; this is what faith provides. Faith in God has sustained me through every step of the legal journey.

The next chapter is about faith, discipline, and longevity which I intend to use to help explain why I am so confident in this journey.

CHAPTER 14

DISCIPLINE, LONGEVITY & FAITH

It has been 11 years since I have touched a monitored phone. There may come a time when I must make use of them, but so far, I have been disciplined enough to stay away from them. The average person that needs to use the phone to survive in here, would not understand the discipline and self-restraint that it takes to accomplish this. Why don't I call my loved ones? What is wrong with writing letters? I do not want to contribute to the prison industrial complex benefit from my family because I do not have the patience to write letters, which I feel are the best way to communicate.

I see myself as a leader. In this position, I do not engage in self centered acts. What I do, is encourage others and give positive advice. I know that kind words can lift spirits out of a somber place. It is extremely difficult unselfish people in a place such as this. Due to the fact that longevity is a major piece of my strategy to make it through, I am determined to stay focused and dedicated to the daily activities that I engage in and who I spend time with.

I keep my circle very tight with the few that I have seen the same discipline that I have in me. They understand that I wake between 4 and

4:30am to keep on track with my personal prayers as well as tending to the spiritual connection between God and I. My God has allowed me to believe that any day, the impossible will be made possible and those who have doubted His amazing truth will finally be awakened by his works.

His grace has given me peace in my mind that has allowed my faith to grow in God.

CHAPTER 15

PEACE OF MIND

"Indeed, they belch with their mouth;
Swords are in their lips;
For they say, 'Who hears?'
But You, O Lord, shall laugh at them;
You shall have all the nations in derision." (Psalm 59:7-8)

I have never lost any sleep due to this wrongful conviction. The reason is that I have always been at peace with God. He has always kept me secure with a peace of mind that helps me do this time. There has to be a spiritual connection because as I have noted, the simplest of things stress people who are doing time. It is a blessing not to be bothered by the hot water being turned off, when there are no showers, phone, or mail.

My faith calms the sea when things are storming in here. my peace allows me to know that everything will be fine. I had to use self-control and discipline to experience the high spiritual power and connection with God. I encourage all that do not believe in his power to seek it with all your heart. What do you have to lose by making a connection with God that could awaken the deep sleepers?

I give this testimony, since my incarceration on July 14, 2010, I have kept a peace of mind which I have faith will continue as I move protected by His grace. I seek His company because there is no other feeling like this. I devote time every morning to read the Word, and I say a little prayer giving thanks and praise. If God helps the ones who do not know Him, what do you think He does for those who do know Him? He is merciful, forgiving, and protects all. I encourage those who do not know him to seek the power that can move mountains.

Peace of mind is powerful! It affords me the strength to make me feel as if my sentence was 2 years. Most people that learn of my case do it via propaganda and form some kind of an opinion, but when I meet people typically cannot believe how relaxed and stress free, I am handling this journey. I know that life is a roller coaster that has ups and downs the whole way around.

I know that my life has a calling upon it and I keep my head up high, because I have made the decision that many will have to make…Heaven or Hell? With peace in my mind, I chose the former. Once I tapped into the spiritual connection, my worries, troubles, hardships, and doubts that I had all went away. This is because He has heard me and will continue to hear me while bringing happiness to my life.

The next chapter focuses on a television show that began airing new cases in 2017. This brand of broadcasting blinds the public from the truth while putting out to potential jurors the state's side of the case. With propaganda being viewed by the public, can anyone have a fair trial? Let us discuss the issue and examine the flaws.

CHAPTER 16

PROPAGANDA

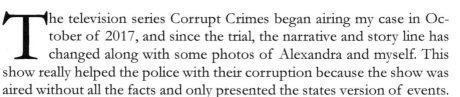

The television series Corrupt Crimes began airing my case in October of 2017, and since the trial, the narrative and story line has changed along with some photos of Alexandra and myself. This show really helped the police with their corruption because the show was aired without all the facts and only presented the states version of events. An investigation into this matter is warranted because what shows like Corrupt Crimes is doing is putting material out there that is not factual and presenting it as though it is factual.

If they were aware of the flaws in the case and still aired it knowing that the investigations were staged and evidence fabricated, the amount of damage that is being done to fair trials is measured in wrongful convictions. This happens in many high-profile cases, and shows like, "The Truth About Murder," hosted by Sunny Hostin, focuses on interviews with the family members of the victims but do not have all the facts to do a complete and just story about the cases.

Sunny Hostin reported on my case, but never mentioned that there was withheld evidence, false and misleading evidence which was used to obtain a wrongful conviction against me. I have to ask why she was used as a puppet? Was her intellect undermined by being made a fool of by officials that had a vested interest in closing this case by wrongfully convicting me?

I beseech you Sunny to start a conversation about the injustice that infects the criminal courts across the country. You have a unique understanding of both sides of criminal proceedings and what conduct would be considered a violation of ethics, due process, and justice. As we are still living in a world that collectively watches police commit murder upon black and brown bodies, the truth about what happens in courtrooms must also be brought to light. The fact that there are bad actors with the power to strip freedom who are engaging in corrupt acts needs to be acknowledged.

Justice is being subverted in courtrooms. I am voicing this to awaken people from slumber to see and act to stop the injustice that is happening in courtrooms every day in this country. What can be done about the show Sunny? Can you take back the interviews that you did? Can you acknowledge that my case was brought to your attention based off the corruption and that I did not receive a fair trial?

I have detailed the violations and reasons as to why I did not receive a fair trial. This case has been aired to the public, but the public did not get the truth. Sunny, how would you feel if this were your case and you found out what was done to me? My name was and continues to be dragged through the mud as the case airs over and over to the world in an unfair manner that concluded that this case was properly solved and closed.

This is wrong, and from what I can gather from your work, you can not sit idly by as this injustice continues because of your integrity. I might be wrong, but I would have to disagree with myself because you discuss these kinds of issues on Soul of a Nation. So again, I ask, did I receive a fair trial? I think not, and I would be open to discussing all of the wrong that has been done to me throughout this time. Someone indeed needs to be held accountable for the corruption that was involved in this case and the truth must be told.

The first five chapters of this book prove to any state attorney that my case was handled in an unfair manner and orchestrated in a way that the verdict would be in the states favor. The statements that were made up by Anthony Pugh do not add up. There were bloody shoe prints around the victim and throughout the basement where the crime took place. If I wore a body suit as the state's theory claimed, then there would not have been bloody shoe prints going every which way at the crime scene, and the Milford Police Department and the state would not have withheld this favorable evidence.

So why did they withhold this evidence? This is the question that casts doubt on the conviction and adds suspicion on the case overall. If anyone can make an argument and state the facts of this case, it is you, Sunny. I am reaching out for your help. I believe that you can get the truth to people. I do question the shows name, The Truth About Murder, when the true facts of the cases are not being told to the public. I encourage deliberation from those who have read this book. You decide if what has been done to me is fair or not.

It is unfortunate that the unfortunate never get to use their own voice to speak up after their proceedings in court. The abuse of power within the judicial system was designed to silence any corruption so that it remains buried from the people of society. This is so that understanding and real truth can not be found. My intention for writing this book is to shine a light upon my incompetent case and to give information about the corrupt tactics that the police and the prosecution use by employing propaganda to keep society blind so they can paint a guilty picture of the unfortunate.

There are three shows that televise my case; Corrupt Crimes, The Truth About Murder hosted by Sunny Hostin, and True Crimes hosted by Nancy Grace. These shows were used as tactics by the police and prosecution in keeping the public blinded to the propaganda schemes. There is a saying which states that the truth always comes to the light. So, I ask, does anyone reading this book see what I see? Is it odd that the police and prosecution went so hard on my case? Showing it so much as they had to get a certain narrative out, so that when the truth was heard, it would sound so odd…as though they were trying to hide something.

For those who never had the courage to fight or to speak up about your case, I encourage you to awaken from your stagnation and help yourself because no on is going to fight as hard as you for yourself. I have witnessed the unfortunate go through plenty of law firms assigned by the state which ensures that the attorney shell game is played which keeps the unfortunates stuck in the system.

I will not allow myself to be a victim to this modern slave organization. It took one time to understand that I did not want this situation for myself. I quickly came to understand that I will not be a part of this process or a statistic to this problem. To combat this stall tactic, I have created a PayPal campaign to help me pay for a law firm of my own choosing, instead of the state controlling my life.

I had to shake off what was done to me by a law firm that was assigned to represent me in my Habeas Corpus proceeding, but the attorney from this firm who gave me her word that she saw the corruption and would get me back in court abruptly left the case and me high and dry. I believe that the state got to her and forced her to break her word to me. Imagine someone going through this four to five times or more. This is a modern slave trade game that the state plays with our bodies and lives. Society is not aware of this however because it is not mentioned or acknowledged to the public.

For those who are doing time, I say to you—Wake up! Help yourself! Use your time to think outside the box and find a way to help yourself escape from modern day slavery.

CHAPTER 17

IDEAS, ACCOMPLISHMENTS, SUCCESS

What is an idea? What are your accomplishments? How do you interpret success? My idea is creating something that can be discussed with the creative mind and understood by others. This allows for a conversation about the truth so that the ones that do not believe can start to comprehend how easily a corrupt official can destroy a person's life by abusing their power.

My mind has allowed me to vividly portray in this book how I was able to recognize the corruption within this investigation. Case and point, what was done to me was unfair. This book came to me from an idea that I wanted to be able to bring knowledge to the people who had no clue about my case, and also to bring awareness to the upstanding people that are in a position of power that can create change.

There are those who believed that they knew the truth about my case, but they were disrespected by their colleagues who withheld facts and prosecuted the case as if everything was done correctly. I do not blame anyone that had been kept in the dark about the corruption, but here is where a difference can be made. Now, all have been made aware of the issues. It is my hope that more oversight will be activated so that stricter punishments can put corrupt state attorneys in handcuffs and fairer ethical practices can be implemented across the board.

Success is easy when your mind is focused. It begins with ambition and deep motivation. I blocked out all negative thoughts that had begun to creep in on the day of my sentencing. I have made it my duty to get my point across to the people so that it can be understood that it does not take a person that is in the legal field to understand the errors that were committed in my trial. One only has to be attentive to their surroundings and checkmate the process.

Success to me is like playing chess. If you are not paying close attention to your opponent, then you will not be able to achieve your victory as your strategy will ultimately fail. I say to the ones who doubt—Imagine That, which is the next chapter, and it will continue to keep you shocked by the pure generous heart of mine, that most people could never imagine to be true.

Before I go into Chapter 17: Imagine That, I want you to think about what an idea can do for you and the change it can bring to turn misery into positive success. I can tell you all of the ideas that I have created but I invite you to tap into your greatness and challenge yourself to do better. This is not hard to do, but it requires you to believe in yourself when others may not.

As a matter of fact, give yourself a reason to prove to others that you are far from the level that they think that you are on. Your ideas, accomplishments, and success will be a light to others. So, I say again, give yourself more credit than you are giving yourself now, and change the game, your life, your negativity to positivity and this will form a better connection with your surroundings in life.

CHAPTER 18

IMAGINE THAT

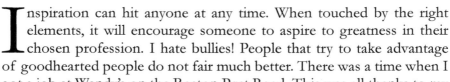

Inspiration can hit anyone at any time. When touched by the right elements, it will encourage someone to aspire to greatness in their chosen profession. I hate bullies! People that try to take advantage of goodhearted people do not fair much better. There was a time when I got a job at Wendy's on the Boston Post Road. This was all thanks to my second cousin, Gus, who was the manager at the time. We worked well together, and we were close like family should be.

One night, Gus had a problem with two former employees who were from the streets. They called Wendy's and began speaking very disrespectfully to Gus. I could see that he did not want any problems, but at the same time I could not allow these guys to disrespect my blood. I snatched the phone and told the two guys that if they had something to say then they should come talk that B.S. to my face. They wanted to know who I was, and I responded by saying come and find out.

Gus could not believe that I did that for him, but I could still see that he did not want any problems. Gus started to joke and tell me of the times that they would bluff by saying that they were on their way, but they never came until this time. When they arrived, I just knew that what was about to happen would not be forgotten by Gus or his adversaries. Once the guys started yelling at the door, Gus and I punched out and went to the door. I asked Gus if he was ready, and he gave me the light. I pushed out of the door.

I focused on the tall slim kid standing about 5'8 or 5'9 that was talking too much. I had enough of this, so I took a silent but strong step to his face. My fist connected perfectly, and he fell to the ground knocked out cold. Gus had never seen anyone get knocked out before, so he was watching me and not my back. When I went for the guy knocked out on the ground, I felt a hard thump across my back. My adrenaline was so fired up that the strike did not phase me. Gus jumped up from his crouching position and was on the kid who hit me with a baseball bat.

I tell this story not to glorify senseless violence, but I tell it to say that inspiration can come from anywhere, as this incident ignited the ambition that lay dormant within Gus. He went on to learn how to box so that he could protect himself and his surroundings. My cousin is now a professional boxer and trains the youth so that they can protect themselves in this cold world.

Imagine yourself with enough discipline and self-control to stay out of trouble while living in a hostile environment in which every morning that you wake up in a very tight cell with another person that you may or may not have a good relationship with. It could be imagined that this would indeed be an extremely uncomfortable situation. I came here to say that it can actually be accomplished. No matter what the situation and institution may present.

I have been ticket-free since the start of this incarceration of July 14, 2010. These eleven years have tested me, but I have passed each of these tests because I know how to move in here and have always kept my circle tight. The state receives funds to offer programs to inmates so that a chance to better oneself is available. More often than not, these programs fail because they lack the main ingredient that would give the people the tools that are really needed to know the person they really are. What is missing is leadership training.

I was offered a chance at becoming a mentor to the youth in the program that they have at this facility. I turned down this opportunity because my beliefs were in contrast to the ones that made up the program. I believe that a program does not have to control a person's surroundings or the way that they live in order to achieve great results in personal growth. What the system is lacking is a system that evaluates all people based on how one gains and uses knowledge, wisdom, and understanding.

The way that one reacts to something in a situation should matter. I believe that the youth can gain personal growth by seeing, understanding, and implementing the works that leaders around them display.

I have an idea for inmates who are tired of the Bull***t and who are never leaving the path of self-improvement. The idea is simple. Anyone who stays ticket-free for 10-15 years will receive a single cell which is the most coveted status in the prison system. It is a challenge to stay ticket-free for this long and the sacrifices that are required for this are plentiful, but it is possible. My idea was taken well when I pitched it to the staff and the long-term changes that would have had to take place were clear. The peace that would come over the prison would be felt by all because, really, who would not strive to obtain and keep a single cell? The stick point is that the system does not give a damn!

The system wants violent inmates and unbecoming behavior to fester within these walls because it is not only job security but also a reason to employ police tactics of brutality which uses excessive force against an inmate when any force in their eyes is deemed necessary.

I believe that anyone can make a change in their life. If programs on leadership became available, the participants in the programs would gain confidence that will inspire change. Within these programs, tight circles based on trust would be formed where discussions of success, discipline, and adulthood would occur, and experiences shared with the goal of people being healed. Programs like this are needed because it is extremely easy for a person to lose hope while trapped within these walls. Within these walls, lives hostile things that do not want change or for any good to happen at all.

For my politicians that are reading this book or leaders that are look ing for change in the prison system, lets begin by implementing the 10% law back to the judicial system for harsher conviction sentences that never give a person a chance to prove themselves back into society. They have all these programs for the youth but yet there is a rise in youthful offenders. The mentors and leaders that are willing to change and make a difference never get that 2nd change because they are considered done to the system.

If there was a 10% second chance to that person's harsh sentence, I think this could be a start to a change and show that this 10% law can open the doors that have been shut on the ones who have lost hope in the judicial system. This law could be written up as a one chance only to a violent crime to give the convicted person a reason to prove that change is possible.

I authored this book to inspire all those who have lost hope. Keep hope and awaken from the slumber. Get your mind right because nothing in life is easy or free, but great things can be done within a lifetime and the person that you were born to be is ready, waiting, and willing to say hello to the world. Find a mentor, become a leader, be a mentor, and make more leaders. You have greatness in you! IMAGINE THAT!

Motivational Song - *"Drown"*
Lacre ft. John Legend

CHAPTER 19

NEVER REGRET

C ompassion is what good will feel like when it encounters suffering. Empathetic joy is what goodwill feels when it encounters happiness. I never had any regrets about the guilty verdict that the jury reached. If I had been found innocent, none of this corruption that infected my trial, and the investigation of the crime would never have been made known to the public. I pose a question to the jurors that returned this verdict. How many times did Eillen Cruz Palarino try to convince you to vote guilty?

If you are reading this book, this is something serious. A juror that admitted that she knew and worked with the deceased's cousin had to have bias and should have been removed from the jury. Some might believe that this is a work of fiction, but this is a true account of what took place in my trial. No one at the time of the trial knew about these disturbing violations that stripped me of my rights as a United States Citizen. If I had not been so focused on the things that were happening in the trial, I could not have written this book, nor would I have been able to keep up my fight for freedom.

I would like to think that A.D.A Amy Bepko did not know of her boss's corruption. The prosecutor Kevin Lawlar showed no fear in using corruptive tactics to obtain a conviction. I thought I saw that A.D.A. Bepko becoming blind to the facts, but corruption blinds and stops people from doing their own investigations and using their knowledge and skill. I say to you Ms. Bepko, with now knowing that there was evidence withheld and other issues that can overturn this case that the state made against me, do you still believe that this conviction is just and correct?

Even if the obvious mistakes are overlooked, people's actions do make a difference. In this case, an action to call out corruption is needed. This is what I am attempting to do within this book. To understand that there is something to learn is the first step to wisdom. One might say, what could a convicted felon teach me? With an open mind, you can quickly learn the basics of knowing a wise man from a fool.

A wise person tends to their responsibilities and avoids the things that they are not. A fool on the other hand, tends to ignore responsibilities and focuses on responsibilities that do not fall upon him. This principal is key in forming your strategy for getting the mind to avoid the things you like to do but will be harmful in the long term. Getting yourself to do the difficult things now will give you long term happiness. I remind myself that I want to be kind to myself and to other people.

I have developed this attitude because it helps my mind to generate a positive attitude ahead of time. For example, no one can tell if they are going to wake up and what their attitude will be. If one programs their mind then, a positive state of mind will be present when you wake up regardless of your surroundings. This is how I think in a comfortable manner and fashion my thoughts and perception to shape a greater sense of wellbeing. This, for me, is the start of patience and the time to utilize the powers of observation.

This is what I used to see the corruption and loopholes that were being played out in the courtroom. For those who participated in the case or watched the case, I ask why weren't the things that I noticed somehow noticed by all of you? Did you all notice and turn a blind eye in compliance with obtaining a wrongful conviction? Never Regret.

Regardless of how the wrong done to me is analyzed, the wrong has been done. Bias from the prosecutor was evident and proven when he made the comment that they would never go into my hood or neighborhood which stereotyped me as a menace to society. The truth was that the prosecutor was the menace to this trial, and he disrespected the judge, jury, his own team, and me. This all added up to violations of my Due Process and Constitutional rights.

This is my reason for writing this book, to let the truth be known. 2015 is over and corruption and corrupted officials are headed the same way. These deceptive actions will have consequences. Never Regret!

I have laid down the cutting edge of truth that can help one become aware of their surroundings and achieve a peaceful state of mind no matter what the circumstance may be. Freedom, respect, and family should never be taken for granted. This trinity is the serenity that keeps my mind at peace.

CHAPTER 20

FREEDOM, RESPECT & FAMILY

What most might not understand is when I was handcuffed at the sentencing hearing, I felt my freedom stay intact because I saw and acknowledged the violations happening and knew that there had to be a way out. The professionals counted me out and could not give credit to the way that my mind was working and observing the trial. I had patience to get to a Habeas trial where all will be exposed.

The system has a plan for those who are incarcerated. Their plan is to make prison a sufferable place. I want to teach you a process to keep your freedom while behind these walls. Keep yourself busy and make yourself useful. The mindset of violence and ignorance is going to make doing time harder. This does not mean you have to play by the rules. The technique is to do you and stay out of the way, but always keep a plan and never put yourself on hold.

This journey has taught me to keep my circle tight and to never pay any mind to those who do not make any sense and do not seek unnecessary attention. A leader will understand the process for staying stress free and how moves should be made. I wake up the same way every morning with a positive attitude. I keep my relationship with God strong and I acknowledge others in a respectable manner. I see no reason to switch it up. I know myself and there is nothing to prove to anyone and my only focus is on getting back home to my family.

If you feel that this is too hard to handle, then possibly the mindset that is employed is already compromised and progression is stalled with negative thoughts. I could have been angry throughout this entire journey, but common sense lets a wise person see that anger will only worsen the circumstances. If violence is a weakness in your life, avoid it like the plague and any thing that may trigger your anger. Practice this by conversating and having consideration for the next person. By keeping these techniques, respect will always be around you.

Respect is either earned or taken, and those who take it normally do not survive because they are forever looking over their shoulders. If respect is earned, you not only enlighten the ones around you, but you also show yourself as a teachable lesson to those that are clueless on the ways that respect is earned.

I wrote this book in hopes that my adversaries come to respect my comments of truth because this book is brought about by leadership and by thinking outside of the box. I did not want this book to be another one of those books about court proceedings that usually bore the reader and loses the readers attention. My intention is to give the reader a different perspective about what really goes on in a person's mind when they are sentenced in a court of law and then are confined to a prison.

Life still goes on in a sense, in a way that is completely different from what has been the norm for so long. There are obstacles and tribulations that one will need to overcome but these are the stepping-stones of life and the way to success in life.

I have been disrespected by some that were by my side in life, and they have done very disrespectful things which I view as personal violations. I have learned to forgive them; I can't let hatred hang around my neck like a weight that I cannot remove. Instead, I show how my inner peace has given me knowledge to grant forgiveness to those who have wronged me. I will not name you in this book. I will make it my business to have a conversation with you to gain some clarity as to why, and at the same time acknowledge that it did not block my blessing. I did not lower myself to your level.

Some people never understand that there are levels to a person's character, and a person cannot be judged by what they say but rather, it is their actions that tell the truth. If this is kept in mind and one carries this as a trait, I can promise that there should never be a question of the ones who you allow into your circle. The circle that I keep around me is flawless and there are no problems with communication or learning from one another. Respect has to be earned not taken. Once earned, you will see a significant difference in how relationships form into a sincere bond.

When a person reaches this level, they are considered family. This is the reason that there is so much distrust among associates. There was never any respect to begin with. It clearly felt that people at my trial wanted me to suffer. I did not have any family members at my trial so there was a falsity being told that I was left for dead. The truth of the matter was I told my family not to appear at my trial.

I did this because I felt that I was in control, and I did not need any physical support in the courtroom. There is no breaking the bond that the Pugh family is held by. The love and support have always been upon me since I was in my mother's womb. I can be misjudged on many things but the love for my family is not one of them. Due to this love, I have received a gift that keeps me shining when darkness surrounds me.

I not only have a biological family in the world, but I have established a family behind these walls. Most will find it hard to believe that I could find anyone in prison that would be worthy enough for me to call family, but those are the ones who mistakenly feel that they do not need anyone and have no respect for friendship.

I am just waiting to be released due to the wrongful conviction that the state obtained. Bill Cosby being released due to the prosecution failing to honor their words and turn a blind eye to justice to obtain a conviction at any cost has given new determination to my fight for freedom. Mr. Cosby stood his ground. He said he was innocent from day one and rejected a sex offenders class offered to him as an essential program that he would need to make parole.

Mr. Cosby rejected the class as well as the hope of parole because he could not admit to something that he was not guilty of or break under the pressure of the hopes of making parole. Due to his strength and belief in himself, the Supreme Court of Pennsylvania spoke loudly and shocked the world with their decision in the case, which was to free Mr. Cosby.

I have to believe that if Mr. Cosby would read this book that he would understand the circumstances that I speak about because he was also sent to prison by a wrongful conviction, just as I was.

Family is all about love, support, leadership, trust, communication, power, acceptance, strength, dedication, discipline, positive mindset, and keeping family first. If you apply these qualities to your circle, there is no way that the bond created could ever be broken, destroyed, or diminished.

EPILOGUE

What have we learned from this book?

Simply a technique any person can use in their daily life or going through trials that you have encountered in your path. All you need to do is believe in yourself and you too can prove your point and get the last laugh. This book heightens your vision and awareness of the corruption that can be detected by staying attentive to the signs of deception within the proceedings. This book also contains exercises that will challenge and push you to your limits. Keep seeking that rush.

I wrote this book to help those who have given up the fight and for those who are going through struggles fighting system. Remember, that there is a method to making a situation more manageable. With principals, doors can be opened that will lead to your success, longevity, prosperity, and faith.

Confidence is the key to leadership and movement. Without it, there will be nothing but second guessing of your greatness. If you are seeing the picture that I am painting for you, then you have the mind set to see through the deception to the corruption clearly. I ask that you be silent no more, with your faith and believe that God does help those who help themselves.

I, Matthew Pugh, am asking for the public's help in making my Go Fund Me campaign successful. The goal is $150,000 to aid in my continuing defense. This case will continue to be complex, as will the remaining steps to freedom and the fight back at the trial level. I will continue to expose the corruption that was done to me, proving that my due process and Constitutional Rights were violated. The truth needs to be told. The government officials used nefarious tactics of strategic propaganda to blind the public of the real truth. Your donations to my Go Fund Me will help give me a chance to hire a competent attorney to fight for my freedom that was unjustly taken from me by government officials that corrupted the law and hid evidence in my case. You can donate at: Gofundme/DifferentBreed.com.

God Bless and Many Blessings,

Matthew Pugh

AFTERWORD

"My glory is fresh within me,
And my bow is renewed in my hand.
Men listened to me and waited,
And kept silence for my counsel.
After my words they did not speak again,
And my speech settled on them as dew.
They waited for me as for the rain
And they opened their mouth wide as for the spring rain.
If I mocked at them, they did not believe it.
And the light of my countenance they did not cast down.
I chose the way for them and sat as a chief;
So I dwelt as a King in the army,
As one who comforts the mourners." (Job 29:20-25).

Translation: In the words of Matthew Pugh

My light is bright within me, and my knowledge is expressed with my pen. Many have waited patiently to listen silently to my advice. After reading my book, the truth opened their eyes and mind.

This knowledge, wisdom and understand quenched their thirst as food for thought. The truth hurts, but honestly frees the mind. I wrote this book to help you, as a leader, for those who have lost hope behind these walls.

Tap into your Greatness.

Who knew how powerful a conversation could be? A simple idea grew between Matthew Pugh and Kevin Epps during a brainstorming session. The focus was on how we could help ourselves, our families, and our communities. Some might ask why we would be thinking about things like this, but these are the people who are stuck in their own selfish ways or trying to do things by themselves. These are people who do not want to pass their blessings onto others who may need the help.

If these people would stop blocking their own blessings, the mind could be opened so that understanding of this idea could start to grow within. The chance meeting of the person who has the resources to bring your vision to live could be passed by because the feeling that one holds may be that no on is to be trusted. An idea can go but so far when it is trapped in the mind but planning, trust, ambition, and a simple conversation can allow a foundation to be built, so that greatness can be tapped into.

This is how our business gets executed. We will never allow these walls to hinder our growth! I want to encourage others doing time to see what might be impossible is actually really possible. I encourage those reading this book to understand that Epps and I, did not let this time defeat us. We use time constructively in our quest to our ourselves and others seeking greatness.

Trust and remember that God helps those who help themselves. "Tap into your Greatness," and receive your blessings for yourself, your family, and your community.

Motivational Song - *"Having our way"*
Migos/ Drake

Prayer to be of Service

Infinite intelligence allows me confidence, health, happiness, prosperity, and well-being to help those who have lost hope to establish better awareness for their spiritual guidance that will spark that light for clearing away the darkness in their path towards obtaining tranquility and to have peace of mind with ambitions, goals, achievement, and success.

Many Blessings,
Matthew Pugh
AKA Breed

Family Roots

If you look deeply into the palm of your hand, you will see your parents and generations of ancestors. All are alive in this moment, each is present in your body. You are a continuation of each of these people.

FREEDOM. Respect. FAMILY.

Recognition

I am grateful to receive this leadership from being connected to my spiritual source which allowed divine people that inspired me to write this book.

My mother, father, brother, sister, children, and big bro Solomon, Gus, Cali Grandmother Lossie Pugh (R.I.P), Grandmother Eva Moye (R.I.P), Grandfather Earl Moye (R.I.P), Saadiq, Slim, Blue, Jon Jon, Dolow, Tim, B.G., Fatty, Moe Diz, J.B, Mustafa, Charise T., Mariam D., Audrey, Chase, Da Original D-Mac, Nat, Corrinna S., 3-25, Grandchildren, Neice and Nephew, Attorney Priya Kiran (for seeing my vision), Teddy C. AKA Slice, and Tasha 3-31 for supporting me at trial. Lisa G, Jermaine Gumbs, Sonja Fitz, T-Lee, Drex, Alpha Delta Family, Herman Green (R.I.P), Tony Green, June Green, Cleco, Job, Vinny aka V (R.I.P) Drip, L.C., Stormi, D.E.X, Poopie aka Tru Bubski, Brett, Dman, Mike, Roy, Troop, T-Base, Mizzy Dread, Budda, D. World, Dave, P.Fox, Meat (R.I.P), Riznut, Compton, Flex, Monica, Shelly, P.L.O, L.Q (R.I.P), Wanda, Betsy, Ardy Bro, Ace (R.I.P), Gary, Slick, Lee, Sean, Gwen, B.V.D, P.I.G, Vanessa Hobby, Darryl Cooper (R.I.P), Lil D-Mac, Porsha, Barbara, Joan, April, White Rock (R.I.P), Anna, Sharren, Maria, S.I.P (R.I.P), Mike, Freddy, Whitey, Get Rich, M1 Lex B.Gizzle, Jessie, Sage, Dip, G.Bo, Yayo, Marlone Johnson, Fletcher, Von, Macho, Keith, June, Loue, Yak, Remy, Dice, Q.B, Hood, D.V, D.Bev, G. Snook, Hasam, Ninja, Soas, Ghost, Rell, X, R.O Bezo, Philly, Mock, Solo, M.J, Colt, Cash, Skill, Ren G, Chino, Fuk, E, Eric, Clark, Pound, Yoshi, Jay, Mike, N.Y Great, Brett, Taylor, Tote, Malik, Rasheed, Jay-y, P, E, Kenny Cropper, Anthony Johnson, Leslie Naduk, Kelly Wade, Shawna Johnson, Kasha McKnight, Paul Deluca, Danielle McKnight, Melissa, Jonathan, Nikki, Laranda Stanley, Zamara, Jessica, Angel, "Keisha, kia, Melinda," 2nd cousins, Evelyn, Iasha, Teli, Nikki, George, Sunka, Kim Blanks, Eric Watts R.I.P, Monique Moye R.I.P, Aunt Delorse R.I.P, Rasper Pugh Jr. R.I.P, Rasper Sr. R.I.P, Aunt Ingrid R.I.P, Uncle Ray Pugh R.I.P, "All Prison Reforms For Change."

In addition, I would like to recognize the following people:

Manio Twins – Troy and Dana, Darky B, Jonny J R.I.P, Pone; FlyTy, Tru, Hube, J-Rocca, Twizzy Chuck, Blue Tape, I.C.U., West, Sherman Brown, G. World, D. Nice, Shan Black R.I.P, Bubski, Danielle, Tameka, Evette, Fransheska, D.V, DayDay, Nathalie, Richlin M, Caprise W, Janet, Red, Wee Wee, Joe, Grande, Q, Trey, Cell, Gail T, Trey Streeter, Trav, Hell Rell, Ricky R.I.P, L.B. R.I.P, Bo Flash R.I.P, Earth, R.I.P, Nitty, Star Nitty, Nina D, Sleepy, Repo (Silvia), Tree, Kia Rodney Jenkins, Torrance F, Tonika L. Rob, Tina, Stephanie, Bobby Wiz, Ray, Jeff, Deacon Davis, Isabel, Rod, Phil, MilliRoc, Dean, Karen C, Chino, Bill "Taught me how to be a molder", Twiz, Roach, Mingo, Lady Red, Ned Carlos, Nisha, Tatum, Jazz, Peanut, Natasha, Denise, Tanya, Lisa, Pinky, Snow, Pittman, Vern, Jennifer, Jessica, Ketty, Maria, Sharon, Kareem P, Darshell P, Lashawna S, Cynthia M, Squeak R.I.P, Joan B, Melissa B, Hefi, Hov, Chic, Tone, Tony, Phil, Jones, Bobby, Kike, Ruben, Stacy C, C. White, Lil Doo R.I.P, India, Sandra, Jeff, Hoodie, Mikey Bone, Heroin, Paul, Jose, P, Susan From the Nissan Dealership, Mike Streeter, Hustle 2.0, Reverse Sympathy, Gordo, Charlie O, Barrack, A.R., Alyssa, Christy, Poppie-Patricia, Flaco, Ray-Ray, NAP, Black, Mally J, Jerrik, Doughboy and Brother, Wan, Peso, Ant Live, Mel, Moan, Donut, Marquise, E.J., D.L., Crystal A, Crystal J, Danika, Rick, Nessa, Glo, Michelle D, Keisha, Irma, Judy, Ben, G. From West Haven, Donna, Russel Fuji, Janene, R.C., Mase, Kaos, T.S. R.I.P, J. Vonn, Kiki, Mike Smitty, Mike Miz, FAB, Darnella, Deanna, Lonnie, Danny, L.O., Todd, Josh, Mush, TAZ, Snoop, Dreep, Leon's Barber Shop, Sonya G, Nicole G, Caroline G, Miranda, Veronica, Chris Cole, Gabe, Kim, Thadius, Shirley, UZI, Vivianna, Passion, VAL, Faye, Kendra, Monique, Jazzy, Joyce, Leslie, Shanghai, Crack, Arlette, C.L., Catfish, Tina F., Jamaican Karen, Gucci, Mass, Delone, Shanita, Fuzz, Spook, F.B., Chocolate, Cory, Jared Green, Moya, Eva, Niomi, Carmen V, Shelly, Tory, Monica, Nikki L, Blaze, Mike S, Timothy P, Rodrick B R.I.P, Hope, Laura, Cami, Bart R.I.P, James F, Roc, Greg, Jamaica, Bug, Bub, Terry T, Cathy T, John Tudor, R.I.P, Choc, White Bay Vinny, Potus, Ali Doo, "Malik" AKA Abdul, Louis V, O.G. Carl From Dwight St, Kool Aid, Fat Vic, Doughboy Jim, Laronda S, Heru, Mack Diamond, John Tucker, J. Money, Mase, Mooney, Double R, Tyson, Greyheart, Dana AKA Pinky, Rick, Wood, Megan, Delora, S. Blaze, Lisy, Jody, Tyler, Joe Pat, Gary Gates, Charlie, Emoji, Harold's Barber Shop, Billy, Uncle Bill R.I.P., Bishop Parker R.I.P., Plashette Perry, Tory, Kim, Janieva, Silvia, Dana, Michael, Chamira, Michelle B, Keith, Cotten's Barber Shop, Megan Perry, Nitro's Clothing, Alpha Delta Family Pizza, Hope H, Frank White.

To my adversaries that gave me the drive to fight for the truth to be exposed.

I See Through Your Corruption
Therefore
I WILL BE SILENT NO MORE!

To all that know how to move behind these walls and have a plan to execute, upon their greatness towards success.
Each life has a fount filled with jewels of wisdom to prosper from. My fount was filled by:

Mustafa "Fresh ones Barbershop"
Devon "Elephant in the room boxing"
Sandra and Miguel "Sandra's Next Generation"
Bernard "R.I.P," Moe, Meat, Boo, Warren
Mike Cooper
Celest Jones
Mr. Barber "Track Coach"
Ray Boyd
Pep "Nitro's Clothing"
N.Y.C Bill and Chris
Dominican Blondie
Da Original D-Mack
Will aka Chill
Bobby aka B.O.B
Troy aka Woody
Marcus aka Cavey
Sheema
Will aka Swallow
Double O, 5'8
Jamaican Steve
George B. aka GB
Jun Boy
M.D R.I.P. A TRUE LEGEND on Kensington St.
Ms. Sumpter "Teacher from co-op high school"
Martial Art Dave
Cathy-I turned down over half a million dollars to help another person that was in need but thank you for the offer.

David Bailey AKA TRU
Troy Streeter
Dave White
Darryl Perkins "Barber"
Michael Smith "Cousins to LL Cool J"
Diane Cropper "Maryland"
Pete "Supervisor, Chromally CT."
Larry Tillman
Connie Streeter
Gengiz "Boss at Alpha Delta Pizza"
Uncle Buck
Chuck Brewer aka "Pastor"
Wink C
Mark Evans aka Biz
John Belton
Bam Bam
T-Lee
Scott X
Baby Mocha-Thank you for giving me the Power of Positive Thinking (The Book) when I need it most. Much Love Sis.
Terry Harper
Desirea Brooks and "Sister"
Holly Texteria "Probation Officer"
Vernice Davis "Choir Instructor"
Rachael "Keeps positive energy"
"U Don't Know Me"-For your leadership and thoroughness
Scott "Thanks for the nutrition college book"
Ice-Your actions display your realness and calm demeanor
Ms. Cozy - "For your confidence and kind personality as well as a great listener."
Technician M.A. for your steady hands and positive drive.
Pastor Parker - leader for Sweet Hope Church
Dr. D & Dr. M - for keeping my health in the greatest level for longevity, youthfulness, and energy.
Pinky - your care helps cure any wounds.

There comes a time in your life that requires you to reflect upon the people that helped you move with motivation, positivity, determination, leadership, and a mindset to win. I would love to thank those that I have mentioned, because of your status, which has levitated my intellect for creative ideas dreamed for the world.

Motivational Song - *"So Ambitious"*
Jay-Z

In this photo there is a total of 613 years and as you can see through their demeanor the fight is still in them. This time has been cut in half from staying focused on their freedom.

Never feel that your patience is running out. Turn your past into success! Stop taking your blessings for granted and proceed with your greatness to a new level you've discovered. Don't wait for the next attorney to solve your issues, show your leadership, and help yourself with your wisdom, knowledge, and understanding. No one is going to fight harder than yourself, so if you want to see a change, wake up and handle your business. This is how I was able to disrupt the corruption with my case. Sometimes you just have to know when to act and expose the truth. Don't be afraid to put yourself in an uncomfortable situation because no matter how bad your adversity may be, you're still overcoming and ahead of those who give up.

You have a choice – what can you learn from it – figure out how to use it as an opportunity.

Opportunity only works if you allow yourself <u>the chance to improve</u>!

-Breed.

BONUS

This is for all those who are unaware of this app that enables you to access your money early. Check out the podcast, "a16z" "The Hustlers Guide to Getting Paid."

I am aware of those who are busy working hard at what you do. It is my hope that this nugget of information will be useful. Knowledge is not power. Applied knowledge is where the power lives.

BREED

"Longevity and Prosperity"
To my neighborhood and community
Support builds character which
brings leadership to help others
follow and lead a better life.
The streets made me who I am today!
I never forgot where I came from!
Pugh Family
&
Moye Family

Through wisdom, this book is written. And by understanding, it is published.

CPSIA information can be obtained
at www.ICGtesting.com
Printed in the USA
BVHW051705040123
655564BV00014B/733